Luisa Capetillo,
Pioneer Puerto Rican Feminist

Nuestra Voz

S E R I E S

Deborah Cohen
General Editor

Vol. 4

PETER LANG
New York • Washington, D.C./Baltimore • Bern
Frankfurt am Main • Berlin • Brussels • Vienna • Oxford

Norma Valle-Ferrer

Luisa Capetillo, Pioneer Puerto Rican Feminist

Translated by
Gloria Waldman-Schwartz
with the collaboration of students
from the Graduate Program in Translation,
The University of Puerto Rico,
Río Piedras, Spring 1991

PETER LANG
New York • Washington, D.C./Baltimore • Bern
Frankfurt am Main • Berlin • Brussels • Vienna • Oxford

Library of Congress Cataloging-in-Publication Data

Valle-Ferrer, Norma.
[Luisa Capetillo. English]
Luisa Capetillo, pioneer Puerto Rican feminist /Norma Valle-Ferrer;
translated by Gloria Waldman-Schwartz.
p. cm. — (Nuestra voz; vol. 4)
Includes bibliographical references.
1. Capetillo, Luisa, 1879–1922. 2. Feminists—Puerto Rico—Biography.
3. Women socialists—Puerto Rico—Biography. 4. Women
in the labor movement—Puerto Rico. I. Valle-Ferrer, Norma.
II. Waldman-Schwartz, Gloria. III. Title. IV. Series: Nuestra voz; vol. 4
HQ1522.C37 V3513   305.42'092—dc21   99053505
ISBN 0-8204-4285-2
ISSN 1074-6773

Bibliographic information published by **Die Deutsche Bibliothek.**
Die Deutsche Bibliothek lists this publication in the "Deutsche
Nationalbibliografie"; detailed bibliographic data is available
on the Internet at http://dnb.ddb.de/.

Cover image from the April 17, 1922 (page 3) issue
of the Puerto Rican newspaper *Justicia*
Original Spanish version: Valle-Ferrer, Norma. *Luisa Capetillo, historia de una mujer proscrita.*
Editorial Cultural, Río Piedras, Puerto Rico, 1990

The paper in this book meets the guidelines for permanence and durability
of the Committee on Production Guidelines for Book Longevity
of the Council of Library Resources.

© 2006 Peter Lang Publishing, Inc., New York
29 Broadway, New York, NY 10006
www.peterlang.com

To my parents, Victor and Guillermina,
and my daughter, Alana Victoria.
To all the women and men
who have struggled for the
emancipation of women.

Table of Contents

Foreword

From the moment I began my research into the life of Luisa Capetillo in 1974, I was committed to sharing what I learned about her in lectures, conferences and articles. My goal was to place her life and work in the context of the historical period she lived in, alongside her companions, the women and men active in the Puerto Rican labor movement. It is astonishing that Luisa Capetillo lived her life the way she did, at the beginning of the twentieth century. Her progressive ideas and her life-style inspires amazement, then respect and admiration, because of the enormous personal sacrifices she made in order to live a different life and fight for her vision of a new world.

I believe that it is essential, especially for women active in the feminist movement in our country, as well as for those who are affirming their cultural identity, to know about the struggle of Puerto Rican female workers at the beginning of the twentieth century. Luisa Capetillo is a symbol and model to emulate because she was not satisfied with merely having principles and believing in them. She actually lived those principles with an indomitable rectitude, in spite of her contradictions.

I had the privilege of meeting Luisa Capetillo's daughter, Manuelita Ledesma Capetillo, who, although shy at first, soon realized the good faith behind my many questions and was generous to the point of giving me the few belongings she had left of her mother: a small handwritten notebook, some old photographs...I also met her niece, Julie Capetillo de Fair, who was as hungry as I was to know more about her aunt. Two co-workers of Capetillo, Nabal Barreto and Angel Gandía, shared their vivid memories of the labor leader with me. And one day, renowned Puerto Rican scholar, Dr. Margot Arce de Vásquez, called out to me as I was passing the balcony of her youngest daughter's home, to share a Luisa anecdote. When Luisa Capetillo used to visit her father's law office in the city of Caguas, the women of the house were instructed by the head of the household (her father, an attorney) to go inside so they wouldn't have to see the liberated woman wearing pants, who spoke familiarly with the men about public affairs.

I share this book, the first one on the life and work of Luisa Capetillo, with my readers because I believe that there is not enough known
about her work and the work of the women with whom she shared her
historical moment. The archives of the *Federación Libre de Trabajadores
de Puerto Rico* (Free Libertarian Federation of Puerto Rican Workers)
were originally housed in vaults of the central offices of the Federation
in Santurce, during the presidency of don Nicolás Nogueras. When
the Federation was dissolved, the files were moved to his widow's
residence and unfortunately, in 1989, Hurricane Hugo completely destroyed them, including original photos, letters and other documents
pertaining to Luisa Capetillo. Will we ever know what her participation was in the collective bargaining process in the strikes where she
was a leader? How many other letters and documents did she write
that speak to us about her thoughts and actions?

When the importance of the social history of that period is known,
we will also understand the impact and the influence of Luisa Capetillo
on her contemporaries and vice versa. For my part, however, with this
publication, I renew my commitment to continue to bring to light the
history of Puerto Rican women. For as we know ourselves better, we
can more fully identify our role in society.

Norma Valle-Ferrer, 1981
San Juan, Puerto Rico

PREFACE

Translation, Transformation and Transgression

I met Gloria Waldman-Schwartz in Puerto Rico in 1991 during our time as participants in the City University of New York/University of Puerto Rico Intercambio/Exchange Program. An anthropologist myself, and she, a humanities person, we engaged in lively discussions, both theoretical and practical, on the art of translation, and more specifically, on the challenge she and her students faced in "translating" Luisa Capetillo for an English-speaking public, "translating" in the broadest sense of the word: "translating" her life, her sensibility, her words, and the words of biographer, Norma Valle-Ferrer.

I remember her talking about translation as transformation. Any work of translation is a rupture and a transformation. The translator needs to be cautious and daring at the same time. It is a dangerous job, being careful and attentive to both text and context, while being willing to take big risks, break the received categories of one established set, the author's text, in order to create a new set, the translation. The written text is simultaneously an artifact of the author's intimate journey of creation and a historically specific cultural statement about the society and identities in which the author is embedded.

The translator has to be immersed in the specific content of the author's text, cognizant of the historical, cultural, political and philosophical context in which the author wrote—and be fluent in two languages. Especially now, in the era of post-modernism, the concept of the text has been reified. If only the text is real, and only as real as the person who wrote it, then how much more transgressive is the job of the translator, whose duty and task is to change the text.

Translating a symbol/symbolic passage from one language to another required something beyond a strict, literal translation—a new icon had to be identified from within the second language/culture—so the meaning of the symbol, not just its literal cognate, would be presented to the reader. In the case of Luisa Capetillo, the translator(s) wanted the readers to understand and respect the historical specificity of the life and works of this one person, this one unique individual woman, living in Puerto Rico at the beginning of the twentieth century, writing in Spanish, thinking and loving and organizing workers in Spanish. At the same time, the translators wanted to demonstrate her universality, the contemporary relevance Capetillo has for an English-speaking audience in the beginning of the twenty-first century. Quite a challenge...

Another challenge emerged in the course of producing the first draft of the English translation: using the translation project as a group process for a class of graduate students, transgressing more traditional models of pedagogy which would have graduate students engaged in the translation of classical texts, or passages extracted from their context and reproduced in an exercise in translation. In this case, Waldman-Schwartz decided to give the graduate translation class a substantial, significant, never-before-translated book to work with, another level of risk-taking on the part of the professor, giving the task to seeming neophytes, trusting that they would bring something new, fresh, not yet jaundiced and cynical, to the work.

And then there were the cultural/political challenges. The irony here is that while the students were fluent in Spanish, they had little knowledge of the political, anarchist, trade union culture to which Luisa Capetillo dedicated her life. Waldman-Schwartz had to make these commitments and identities come alive for the students, "translating" a world of politics to students with little or no literacy in this domain.

Rupture, violence and aggression are endemic to the work of translation. The received text must be broken apart and then remade, hence, translation as inherently a transgression. Just as Luisa Capetillo's texts were transgressive in her time, so was Norma Valle-Ferrer's text about Luisa Capetillo transgressive when first published in 1990, and so too is the translation of Valle-Ferrer's text that you now have before you.

Gerrie Casey, Ph.D.
Professor of Anthropology
John Jay College,
City University of New York

Acknowledgments

The researching, writing and publishing of a book, as special to me as this one, owes a great deal to many people. I am grateful to all. However, the truth is that this process has been long and difficult and I want to mention a few of those very special people. Dr. Ricardo Alegría inspired and encouraged me. Dr. Luis Nieves Falcón guided my first steps into socio-historical research, while Dr. Guillermo Baralt shared invaluable historical advice. The dedicated employees of the *Archivo General de Puerto Rico* (General Archives of Puerto Rico) were generous with their time and cooperation.

I am grateful to don Nicolás Nogueras Rivera, respected labor leader, and his wife Berta, who shared unpublished letters of Luisa Capetillo and labor leader Santiago Iglesias Pantín with me. Manuel Alvarez Lizardi shared his valuable collection of books about the anarchist movement with me. Reinaldo Ledesma, grandson of Manuel Ledesma, Marquis of Arecibo (father of Luisa Capetillo's first two children), helped me in my search for Luisa Capetillo's daughter.

My heartfelt thanks go to the people who offered firsthand historical testimony about Luisa Capetillo: her daughter Manuelita Ledesma Capetillo, her niece Julie Capetillo de Fair, her son-in-law, José Rosa, and her co-workers, Nabal Barreto and Angel Gandía.

I am grateful to the *Instituto de Cultura Puertorriqueña* and its former director Dr. José Ramón de la Torre for their generous granting of funds to prepare the manuscript in English. This work was also supported (in part) by two grants to Dr. Gloria Waldman-Schwartz from the City University of New York PSC-CUNY Research Award Program to complete the translation of this book into English.

Finally, I give my thanks to Dr. Gloria Waldman-Schwartz for translating this book into English with her students from the Graduate Program in Translation at the University of Puerto Rico; to Petra Hall, who edited the first draft of the translation; and to Jules Feiman, Paul Mishler and Peggy Ann Bliss, for their careful readings of the English manuscript.

Deconstructing the Text,
Reconstructing the Text

The idea of translating the original version in Spanish of this book, *Luisa Capetillo, Historia de una mujer proscrita* (1990) came to me during the spring of 1991, while teaching the course, "Translating Feminist Texts," as a Visiting Professor in the Translation Department of the University of Puerto Rico. It occurred to me that the passionate nature of Luisa Capetillo, her Puerto Ricanness, her politics and her feminism, would make an exciting subject for a class translation project.

The all-female class, women in their 30s and above, were familiar with Norma Valle-Ferrer's groundbreaking book and enthusiastically embraced the project. The book was divided among the seven women and the final class project was to produce a completed manuscript. Similar to my experience with graduates in the Translation Department ten years earlier, when three of them (Myrsa Landrón, Lourdes Morales and Vanessa Rossy) undertook the translation into Spanish of my doctoral thesis, *Luis Rafael Sánchez and the New Latin American Theater* (CUNY, 1979) as their Master's Degree project, these students were also well prepared, insightful and very hard workers.

The translation team included: Carolyn F. Castro Báez, Verónica Cabrera Velarde, Carmen M. Espada, Ivonne López, Zaida M. Negrón, Eunice Rodríguez, and María B. Vásquez Lloréns.

As always with translation, we had to understand the text first, whether that meant deciphering the meaning of the legal documents in the Appendices, or familiarizing ourselves with the specialized vocabulary of nineteenth century anarchism, about which we consulted Norma, and other experts in the fields of social sciences and labor history. After working closely with each student, I believed we had a publishable translation in 1991. I returned to New York, time passed, life happened, and finally in 1999, when Norma came to New York as a

Visiting Professor in the CUNY/UPR Intercambio/Exchange Program, we sat down and reread what we had. Then the second phase of the work began. The translation needed to flow more; it needed tightening; it needed more nuance. This was the task that Norma, editor Petra Hall, and I took on. In 2001, I contacted as many of the student translators as I could find and asked them to share what the project had meant to them. I include excerpts from their reflections.

Carolyn F. Castro Báez

It was a marvelous challenge to work with Norma Valle-Ferrer's book, mainly because of its historic significance. The literal translation was not difficult. The challenge arose in trying to create the same flow and convey the same sensations and images in the translated language, as existed in the original. Once the basic skeleton was established, then came the creative work. It was almost a musical process. It was not limited to the words; we had to work with the sounds and movement of the piece. When we met to polish the translation, it was similar to a jam session.

We would have our dry spells. All of a sudden a spark would come that would ignite the creative process, allowing for a stream of progress, and then back to square one. The more we practiced, the more we were able to proceed continuously, faithfully keeping Norma Valle-Ferrer's signature in the work. Ten years later, I have to admit it is one of the translation experiences that has stayed with me most. I am very excited that it didn't end there, and that Dr. Waldman persisted. If nothing came out of all of the work, I would have felt a degree of shame. Learning about Luisa Capetillo and forgetting about her would be like contributing to the silence that obliterated her in life.

Ivonne López

I felt a great responsibility translating a book about another Puerto Rican woman. I read the whole book and reread my part and translated not only the words but also Luisa's feelings. The group of students that translated the book was small and close. I couldn't see them after class because I had a baby at home waiting for me. It was a very stressful year. I was teaching French full time in a private school. My gifted son was in second grade and my one-year-old daughter was getting sick every month in the nursery. Everybody was stressed out because of the Persian Gulf War. I remember that I had to go to Gloria Waldman's house twice to work on my translation, even on Mother's Day. We all worked hard, but I'm sure that if I had the chance to see my translation again I would change a lot of things. I'm more experienced now and I would find mistakes in style and even choice of words.

Eunice Rodríguez-Ferguson

The dynamic of the project mirrored the ideas underscored in the text; there we were, working as a true sisterhood of collaborators towards a common goal. We grew as professional translators and as individuals. As the class developed our skills and opened our minds, Luisa Capetillo's story continued to be an enduring source of inspiration.

María B. Vásquez Lloréns

My experience in reading, analyzing and translating my part of this work not only made me view modern women from a new perspective, but also helped me understand how women lived and struggled in our recent past, in a world governed by men, a world where public education for girls was not championed by all, a world where Luisa Capetillo would lay the groundwork for a future where women like myself could advance in our personal and professional lives.

I echo the sentiments of my dedicated students concerning the historical significance of the text, the pride and sense of responsibility we all felt bringing this Puerto Rican heroine to life, and the sense of solidarity we shared, working as a group of women on a project with such nationalistic resonance. To their words I add my joy and satisfaction to be contributing to the ever expanding canon of Puerto Rican literature in translation, my way of giving back to the Island that has given me so much over the years: unconditional love and abiding friendships. I would especially like to express my gratitude to Norma Valle-Ferrer for her passion and knowledge and her willingness to share these gifts so generously.

Gloria Waldman-Schwartz
East Quogue, New York

Fig. 1. Handwritten notes, Luisa Capetillo.

Luisa Capetillo in Puerto Rican History

Biographical research on women steadily grew in Puerto Rico during the 1990s and contributed to the creation of our subjective identity as a nation. With the recovery of women's lives we find clues to help us understand ourselves as Puerto Ricans, and as women and men, recognizing that until today, Puerto Rico's national and cultural identity has been analyzed only from a male point of view. Recovering the story of Luisa Capetillo is part of the effort to integrate the history of women into the history of our country.

After this book's first edition was published in 1990, many articles commenting on the life and work of Capetillo appeared in the media. On numerous occasions I was invited to lecture about her writings and about her life. In fact, the irreverent and revolutionary Luisa Capetillo has finally been accepted by those segments of society that in the beginning of the twentieth century ostracized her. Several Women's Studies library collections have been named after her, among them, the Luisa Capetillo Room in the library at the Cayey Campus of the University of Puerto Rico, the Luisa Capetillo Room at the Office of the Attorney General for Women's Affairs in San Juan, and a small library at a co-op in Trujillo Alto. There, children do their homework every day under the scrutiny of Luisa Capetillo, whose photograph looks down at them. Her photo is from the early 1900s but her ideas are as young as the youths growing up Puerto Rican today. Since 2004, an oil portrait of Capetillo by José Rodríguez hangs in the Puerto Rico Capitol in the Senate's *Salón de Mujeres Ilustres* (Gallery of Famous Women).

I was very touched when I read a newspaper article covering the inaugural ceremony of the first woman appointed Chief of Police for the Caimito Precinct in Río Piedras. The policewoman had "tears in her eyes" as she explained to the public that she accepted the challenge of the position thinking of Luisa Capetillo; if Luisa Capetillo could overcome the fiercest obstacles against women's advancement, then she would give it a try in a man's world. Is Capetillo now a popular icon? Maybe. She has indeed become a paradigm for those who struggle for the vindication of the rights of the oppressed.

Luisa Capetillo, Historia de una mujer proscrita is now used as a textbook in several college and high school courses in private and public schools in Puerto Rico. A brief biographical sketch (although devoid of her revolutionary fire) has been included in the textbooks assigned to the required History of Puerto Rico courses in the Puerto Rican educational system—extraordinary accomplishments all.

In 1985, playwright Roberto Ramos Perea and director Edgar Quiles staged five short plays by Capetillo during the Seventeenth Annual Theater Festival of the *Ateneo Puertorriqueño*. The plays were filmed and transmitted at a later date as part of the television program *"El escritor y su mundo"* (Writers and Their World), which Dr. Luis Nieves Falcón hosted on Channel 6, WIPR, one of Puerto Rico's educational stations.

In 1993, filmmaker Sonia Fritz made a documentary drama based on my book. The 42-minute film, entitled *Luisa Capetillo: Pasión de justicia* (Luisa Capetillo: Passion for Justice) has been shown in Puerto Rico and various other countries to critical acclaim. In 1994, it won First Place for Dramatic Documentary in the Latin American Women's Film Festival of Mar del Plata, Argentina.

Luisa Capetillo, Historia de una mujer proscrita belongs to the contemporary cultural phenomenon of women's biographies. Only now are we becoming familiar with María de las Mercedes Barbudo, who struggled for Puerto Rican independence during the eighteenth and early nineteenth centuries and was jailed in El Morro, the infamous military garrison in old San Juan; with Ana Roqué (often referred to as Ana Roqué de Duprey), pioneer journalist and novelist; Carmela Eulate Sanjurjo, travel writer, translator and poet; Librada Rodríguez, labor and political leader; Julia de Burgos, the poet of love and nationhood; and Ruby Black, the United States feminist and First Lady Eleanor Roosevelt's friend and confidante, who made a successful career writing as a correspondent for *La Democracia*, a Puerto Rican daily newspaper.

It is important to note that these biographies are different from the biographical entries that were previously written, focusing only on what was socially acceptable for a woman who lived in a world of men. Biographies today treat the public lives of the women and their contributions to society, not only in their private space but also in the context of their social milieu. The Puerto Rican Association of Historians has made significant contributions to Puerto Rican society with the publication of articles and essays on Puerto Rican women from new perspectives, including the feminist perspective. *Historia y género* (History and Gender, 1997) is a good example of a collection of well written essays on the topic.

Biographies with a feminist perspective are still a challenge to the field of historical investigation in Puerto Rico. We must rediscover the lives of women who have made contributions of an individual and public nature and write their lives from a new point of view. We must find common denominators in the lives of these women who were outstanding in their time and dared to challenge the societies they lived in. We must learn from their values and from their commitment to the future.

Norma Valle-Ferrer, 1998
San Juan, Puerto Rico

Fig. 2. Luisa Capetillo wore pants skirts or harem pants to her union and feminist activities as well as in her private life. This photo
dates from around 1918.

Luisa Capetillo and the Feminist Tradition

During the decade of the seventies, the western world felt the jolt of the new movement to further women's rights, this time organized in a more sophisticated way than during the first wave of feminism at the beginning of the twentieth century. In Europe, as well as in the Americas, the tremor provoked by organized groups of women reached the very roots of society. They were now motivated by a feminist conscience based on a solid theoretical framework and on a history in the process of being written.

Women's history became a focal point for the incipient feminist movement. Women needed to know their past and their origins in order to be self confident in their search for freedom. The 1970s witnessed marches, rallies, the advancement of legal rights, international gatherings and the organization of women into action groups.

In the heat of the feminist movement, institutions to support women were created, such as 24 hour day care centers, sports and recreation centers, enhanced legal and medical services as well as institutions offering educational opportunities. In addition to the practical support of these and other entities, the struggle for female equality demanded that the literature and historical research be narrated by female voices and come from a feminist perspective. The daring and significant paradigms of Mary Wollstonecraft and Olympe de Gouges, the lives and work of feminist socialist theoreticians such as Clara Zetkin and Alexandra Kollontai, inspired women. In every country progressive women and men worked to integrate women's history into the historical canon.

The historical reinterpretation of women's role as home economists, as protagonists in the reproduction of human life and as contributors to moral consciousness must be made visible. The importance of the private and domestic aspects of a woman's life, since that is the world that she primarily lived in for several millennia, must be considered along with her public accomplishments. For this reason when people write about Luisa Capetillo, when they tell the story of her life and work, it is necessary to explain her feelings and her activities as a wife and lover, as a mother and a teacher.

We understand the evolution of Luisa Capetillo's theories by understanding how she challenged the social conventions of her day, by not marrying legally, by wearing pants in public, and in many small revolutionary acts embodied in her daily life. She revolutionized the role of women in Puerto Rican society and became a paradigm for the new woman.

When I initiated my research, motivated by the desire to learn more about the history of Puerto Rican women, I found that everyone who knew Luisa Capetillo when she was alive, or knew about her, remembered her as the first woman in Puerto Rico to wear pants in public. At first I thought these recollections were based on an implied societal intention not to recognize this revolutionary for her important role, but rather to brand her an eccentric, remembered only by what could be considered superficial actions. I was saddened by the fact that even respected intellectuals didn't value her feminist, labor and anarchist work in its true perspective. What I found out was that Luisa Capetillo did not wear pants in public as a whim or to attract attention. She did not preach free love because she was immoral or libertine. She did not become the first feminist in Puerto Rico, both in theory and in action, because she was disappointed in love.

The theories developed by Capetillo and her actions in daily life came from the legitimate theoretical political formation that ruled her life. Luisa Capetillo must be situated in her historical moment. The fact that she was a vegetarian and a true believer in Swedish calisthenics and in yoga, as ways to keep the body in optimum health, has to be discussed. To fully understand this woman, it is not enough to know her intellectual and public accomplishments; how she lived also has to be known.

I did my research at the Historical Archives of Puerto Rico, at the Puerto Rican Collection of the José M. Lázaro Library at the University of Puerto Rico, Río Piedras, at the José Martí Library in Havana, Cuba, at the New York Public Library, and in Ybor City, Florida. I interviewed Luisa Capetillo's daughter, Manuela Ledesma, who provided a deeply felt testimony, Julie Capetillo de Fair, Luisa Capetillo's niece, and various co-workers who still remembered her as a "different woman." I also had the opportunity to examine some letters written by Luisa Capetillo to the labor leader Santiago Iglesias Pantín, in the archives of the

Federación Libre de Trabajadores de Puerto Rico (Free Libertarian Federation of Puerto Rican Workers).

The research and completion of Luisa Capetillo's biography is a work in progress because in Puerto Rico we do not yet have a complete and encompassing history that contextually integrates both the labor and the feminist movements. As this connection is strengthened, important information and insights will be added to the history of Luisa Capetillo, a woman whose ideas were questioned by the traditional society in which she lived, and excluded from its official history.

Fig. 3. Luisa Capetillo (c.1880), approximately one year old.

CHAPTER I

Origins of the Feminist Struggle in Puerto Rico

A woman's right to obtain a formal education can be considered the seminal issue that moved progressive women and men to struggle to the point of challenging the established social system. It is my opinion that women's education was the decisive element that ignited the fight for the emancipation of women because its defenders crossed class barriers, and, if only for a brief moment, there was solidarity between the liberal landowners and the most enlightened elements of the nascent labor movement. As we will see in this chapter, the historical development of female consciousness began to take shape from this significant moment in the second half of the nineteenth century when the bold figure of feminist and anarchist Luisa Capetillo dramatically emerged.

The education of the Puerto Rican woman prior to the nineteenth century depended almost exclusively on the oral and practical education that she received at home from her mother, grandmother, unmarried aunts, and, in the case of families with certain economic means, the female servant. She learned to carry out domestic chores, such as cooking, cleaning and caring for children. Depending on her social status, she may have learned to make clay pots, dishes and utensils for the home, and to work with a hand loom to weave cotton fabrics to make her own clothes.

From a very early age the farm girl began working in the fields, where the family labored to produce food for their consumption. As part of her education she was also trained in various arts and crafts, including sewing, embroidery, ceramics, basket weaving and brush painting. Essentially, a woman's education in Puerto Rico during the sixteenth, seventeenth and eighteenth centuries was not substantially different from the education received by the *Taína* Indian who inhabited *Borinquen* when the Spanish settlers arrived.[1]

The *Taína* woman received her education from the women of the tribe from whom she learned to do farm work, take care of the home, bring up the children, make pottery, weave baskets, and knit.[2] For the black female, who arrived in Puerto Rico as a slave during the sixteenth and seventeenth centuries, work was her entire education; female slaves were used as merchandise, breeders, domestic workers and agricultural laborers. Her mother and the other women in her family taught her to rear her own children and her master's children, acknowledging the inherent disparity between these two social classes.[3]

The Catholic Church, with official government support, made attempts at the beginning of the seventeenth century to establish a convent for Puerto Rican women. The guiding principle behind this project was to provide young girls who lacked dowries, but came from what were considered to be "good families," with a decent occupation, and to enable them to find a husband of sound economic means. The project was not carried out until 1646, when Ana de Lanzós from San Germán founded the Convent of the Carmelite Nuns with a substantial inheritance from her parents. It began with several nuns from the Dominican Republic and three young Puerto Rican women, Ana de Lanzós, her sister and a girlfriend.[4]

Despite the fact that there was no formal education for women, it is possible that during the eighteenth century Age of Enlightenment, some of the women had privately learned what was considered at that time a difficult art—spelling and writing—and had passed it along to groups of young girls. That was the case of María Dolores Araujo, born in 1754, the illegitimate daughter of a "free black woman" who, having acquired formal knowledge in "reading, writing, Christian doctrine and simple sewing," taught various young girls of San Juan for the equivalent of fifty dollars a year.[5] Traditionally, a mother who learned to read and write probably passed her knowledge along to her daughters. María Bibiana Benítez, born at the end of the eighteenth century, was introduced to world literature at a very early age and later became the first woman writer in Puerto Rico. In 1832, she published the poem "La ninfa de Puerto Rico" in the daily government's newspaper La Gaceta de Puerto Rico (The Gazette of Puerto Rico). And in 1843, María Bibiana's niece, poet Alejandrina Benítez, and Benicia Aguayo were the two women that succeeded in publishing their work in *Aguinaldo Puertorriqueño*, the first complete book written and published by Puerto Ricans.[6]

As the nineteenth century progressed, the first teachers from Spain began to arrive in the Puerto Rican colony. On March 6, 1804, four school teachers—Juana Antonia Araujo, Josefa Chavarría, Paula Molinero and Juana Polanco—came to the San Juan City Council to collect their salaries.[7] The *Sociedad Económica de Amigos del País* (The Economic Society of Friends of the Country) also hired a multilingual teacher from the island of St. Thomas to teach different languages to the girls.[8] Discussions ensued with the governor to consider the idea of establishing an academy for young girls. On September 2, 1805, following the example of San Juan, the City Council of Arecibo requested an allotment of one hundred dollars to pay for the expenses of a teacher for young girls.[9]

The sparse education for males and females improved overall as the century advanced. At the same time government leaders enacted legislation regarding public education in the country. On the one hand, public schools were slowly being established; on the other hand, encouraged by government authorities, private schools were being created by independent teachers with a small number of students under their tutelage, supported by the Church and other civic institutions. In 1845, the Economic Society of Friends of the Country granted funds for six scholarships for women and over time substantially increased these funds.[10]

Despite this, schools for females were always at a disadvantage in comparison with schools for males. A census in 1846 revealed that in Puerto Rico there were 74 public schools and 16 private schools for males, and 48 public and 9 private schools for women. The total enrollment for males was 2,376 and 1,092 for women. Of these totals, 2,090 were poor students, who paid no tuition. There were 88 male teachers and 54 female teachers.[11]

In 1859 a Woman's Board was created to establish and manage the San Ildefonso Catholic Boarding School in San Juan for the education and upbringing of young women. The female members of this board not only donated their own money to the San Ildefonso School and collected funds in charity raffles and fairs, but also wrote the by-laws of the school and managed it. In 1867 the school had 73 pupils, both boarding and day pupils. Besides religious studies, students were taught reading, writing and arithmetic. The girls were also instructed in trades that would prepare them to earn their living as adults.[12] Many of them became teachers themselves.

The idea of delegating the responsibility for the education of young girls to organized women's groups became a relatively frequent practice in the history of education in Puerto Rico. In subsequent years, specifically in 1885, Governor General Luis Dabán y Ramírez de Arellano issued a decree approving the By-laws of the *Asociación de Damas para la Instrucción de la Mujer* (The Ladies' Association for the Education of Women). Its goal was to provide professional education and an official degree to young women with a vocation for teaching, with the idea that after receiving their training, they would devote themselves to the education of young girls in public and private schools.[13] This Association in particular, which relied on the patronage of the governor's wife, the Countess of Verdú, was organized in several of Puerto Rico's municipalities. Civic minded women in each town, in cooperation with the local mayor, ran the schools. Governor Dabán y Ramírez de Arellano, who was not known for his diplomacy in his political dealings with either conservatives or liberals, nevertheless succeeded in encouraging primary education for women through these committees.[14]

During the second half of the nineteenth century, advances in women's education in Puerto Rico, at the official level and in private circles, were primarily due to the proliferation of liberal ideas spreading throughout the country among intellectuals who strongly influenced both public opinion and spheres of power, and who vehemently discussed the emancipation of slaves, workers and women.[15] Puerto Rico at that time welcomed liberal philosophies stemming from the French Revolution and subsequently disseminated throughout the Western world. Intellectuals pondered and debated the specific rights and responsibilities of its citizens, male versus female.[16] As their principal argument supporting their defense of women's education, they embraced the idea that society would become wiser and more progressive if women were educated. Since women traditionally have the responsibility of bringing up children, they reasoned that they would be able to create better citizens for the future of the country. As the idea continued to be discussed, experts in the field of women's education joined in, defending women's education as essential to the development of nations. Detractors contended that educated women would create perversion in the world since they would undermine the stability of the traditional family.

Two women—Olympe de Gouges in France and Mary Wollstonecraft in England—articulated some of the initial arguments in defense of a woman's right to an education. Though at that time it was men who prevailed in the world of ideas, some men did indeed speak up in defense of women's rights.[17] As they analyzed and critiqued society, philosophers such as August Bebel, Charles Fourier, Pierre Joseph Proudhon, Frederick Engels, Karl Marx, and William Godwin, used theories of utopian socialism, anarchism, and communism to examine the validity of women's education.[18]

The right to acquire an intellectually rich and free education—including science, until then forbidden to women—became the catalyst which propelled the first known feminists into action. In England, France, and the United States, pioneers of feminism hailed the defense of women's education as a cornerstone of their struggle.[19] Liberal women were inspired to organize the fight for academic education, and liberal men offered their support to the cause. The pattern would repeat itself in almost every western country. Puerto Rico was no exception. The liberal sectors supported women's education, organizing themselves into groups of women to deal directly with the education of their sisters.

The responsibility for the education of women outside the home fell on the private schools, directed by a female teacher, and on the ladies' associations. The By-laws of the Ladies' Association for the Education of Women, drawn up in Lares in 1885, are clear in their statement of purpose:

> Mindful of the remarkable expansion in women's education and instruction in Europe and America, a far reaching movement is being encouraged by individual and societal initiatives, by municipal and provincial associations and by national governments. This Society, under the protection of ladies and young girls of the upper classes, is being established in Puerto Rico with two objectives: one, modest, given the present economic situation that the Province is experiencing, and the other, more ambitious, focusing on the future.[20]

Historian Antonio Cuesta Mendoza confirms my opinion that education was the first issue around which Puerto Rican women organized when he notes, "What a pleasant surprise it is to discover the involvement of the Puerto Rican woman in the meritorious field of education, so long ago, at the dawn of the nineteenth century."[21] This is particularly noteworthy, given the limitations of the Puerto Rican educational system of the time.

There are numerous writers and thinkers in Puerto Rico who echoed the emancipating trends from Europe. Manuel Fernández Juncos, Gabriel Ferrer Hernández, Alejandro Tapia y Rivera, Salvador Brau, Manuel Elzaburu Vizcarrondo, and Eugenio María de Hostos are some of those who made the cause of women's education their own. Fernández Juncos, in the prologue to the book *La mujer* (Woman) by Gabriel Ferrer, adds his voice to the "defense of the emancipation of women," while describing the "gigantic struggle in the world" to achieve women's education.[22] In Alejandro Tapia y Rivera's essay, *"El aprecio de la*

Muger (sic) es barómetro de la civilización" (Appreciation of Women is the Barometer of Civilization), he analyzes societies and civilizations in relation to their attitudes toward women. Tapia says, "Women have been both slaves and free women; they have also occupied the throne of goddesses. But that is not their ultimate end; that is not their path. Women can advance higher and can move towards the natural state by becoming citizens. This is one of the problems that the nineteenth century has to solve."[23]

Eugenio María de Hostos surpassed his contemporaries in his approach to the education of women. While in the Dominican Republic he wrote a series of essays about women's education that he would later present before the Literary Society of Santiago, Chile. In his first speech, *"La educación científica de la mujer"* (Scientific Education of Women), Hostos suggests that the most efficient way to change attitudes and shape a new generation is by educating a woman so that she, as a mother, can convey respect for the truth to her children. "She is all feeling; educate her and our agenda for truth will be achieved through women."[24]

Some of the first Puerto Rican feminists also belonged to this liberal wing; almost all of them were educated in their homes or in small private schools that were run by a single female teacher. Josefina Moll, under the pseudonym of Flor Daliza, states in an essay about women, "Woman, as the eternal inspiration of artists and poets, as muse and as ideal, in the present struggle for her education and betterment, rightfully deserves to be defended by the very ones who demand from her beauty, forms to copy with their chisel and burin, and from her love, sensations that cause the sonorous rhyme and the classic period to spring forth."[25] María Luisa de Angelis and Ana Roqué became well known by organizing feminist groups and publishing seminal documents promoting the advance of women's education.[26]

Regarding the defense of women's education, the liberals concurred with the leaders of the incipient Puerto Rican labor movement, who were already organized into trade unions, artisans' clubs and mutual aid societies, and were busy discussing the vanguard currents promoted by the French Revolution, and later the First Workers International. For reasons that will be discussed shortly, Puerto Rican *campesinos* and artisans from urban centers, in the process of proletarianization since the nineteenth century, began to develop class consciousness and to experience solidarity with the international labor movement. Historical evidence notes that Puerto Rico was influenced by the First Workers International held in Europe in 1866. While the right wing, made up of landowners, praised the socialism of Marx (according to their own definition that differed substantially from the definition of its proponents), and while these landowners probably pretended to adopt certain measures with the outward appearance of socialism in order to appease labor unrest, the Puerto Rican workers themselves leaned towards the libertarian socialism of Michael Bakunin.[27]

It is significant for the history of feminism in Puerto Rico that a majority of the workers and their leaders favored libertarian socialism or anarchism as their guiding philosophical principle for action. It is particularly significant because it was within the ideological framework of anarchism that the most fervent defenders of women's liberation were found, those who were able to put their ideas into practice and implement them, particularly regarding education. Unlike Marxism, which orients society towards a particular political and economic system of government, anarchism was conceived by its originators—Bakunin, Malatesta, Sorel, and Kropotkin—as a "way of life."

In considering anarchism as a way of life, and requiring its followers to live in accordance with their ideology, they are forced to deal with the condition of woman, the natural companion of man, and with the rearing of children, who are the "natural" fruits of man and woman in their "natural" state. As a young man, Marx began to formulate his ideas, and observed, "...the relation of man to woman is the *most natural* relation of human being to human being. It therefore uncovers the extent to which man's *natural* behaviour has become *human*, or the extent to which the *human essence* in him has become a *natural* essence—the extent to which his *human* nature has come to be natural to him."[28] Marx conceptualizes the status of women, but holds it as an abstraction, while the anarchists, on the other hand, embrace the concept, trying to deal with it in practice, since, according to them, only in this way will it be possible to create the new man and the new woman.[29]

Along with theories about "spontaneous revolution" and the organization of *campesinos* and industrial workers into unions and libertarian federations, the anarchists also transmitted a set of ideas about everyday life that included free love and free education, which would result in men and women "free" from conventional ties. The books by Bakunin, Kropotkin and Malatesta (who lived in Latin America for many years), significantly shaped the education of Puerto Rican workers and deeply inspired them. The educational theories of the Catalonian Francisco Ferrer and the French writers Sebastian Fauré and Madeleine Vernet (whom Luisa Capetillo called Magdalena Vernet), became the ideal of Puerto Rican workers.[30]

During the last decades of the nineteenth century, the workers' quality of life deteriorated due to numerous factors, including the transformation of the agricultural economy and its dependence on United States' demands upon its colony (for example, from an emphasis on growing coffee, tobacco, fruits and vegetables, to a massive concentration on sugar cane production), the rise in the cost of living, increased income taxes, and financial crises. During this time, due to a subsequent change in workers' perception of their own reality, a shift also occurred in the paternalistic relations between workers and employers. This in turn, fostered a new proletarian mentality like that of the industrial workers.[31] Dissatisfaction with the establishment provided fertile ground for the anarchists' ideas to grow. In the last decade of the century, sugar cane and tobacco workers participated actively in spontaneous strikes organized and led by José Ferrer y Ferrer, Angel María Dieppa, Santiago Iglesias Pantín, Alonso Torres, Ramón Romero Rosa and others, who in addition to being militant labor agitators in practice, were the ideologues of anarchism and proponents of Bakunin's ideas about organizing women and men workers. These same enlightened workers also theorized in their books and articles about the working conditions of women, encouraging guilds and unions to join forces with the liberals in support of the right of women to have full access to education. Their support was not only for those "young women from good families with no financial means," but also for all women, especially for the female workers and their daughters.

In the late nineteenth century, when Luisa Capetillo was born, Puerto Rico experienced one of the most active moments in the struggle for workers' rights and women's rights. Progressive sectors were stirring and ideas about emancipation were heatedly being propagated. The liberals began organizing into associations that would later form part of the suffragist movement, and the women workers met in guilds and unions to defend themselves against oppression on the job and at home. The defense of a woman's right to education was the motivating and uniting issue which would eventually culminate in a more liberal, complete and progressive education for Puerto Rican women. Tempered by their struggle, women emerged who would lead the feminist movement in the early twentieth century. These women were the liberals Ana Roqué, María Luisa de Angelis, Isabel Andreu de Aguilar, and the workers Luisa Capetillo, Franca de Armiño and Concha Torres. A better and more complete education for women of all social strata remained the unifying cause within the feminist movement throughout the years.

NOTES

1.   See the following anthological histories about education in Puerto Rico, that I found particularly useful: Antonio Cuesta Mendoza, *Historia de la educación en el Puerto Rico colonial* (México: Imprenta Manuel León Sánchez S.C.L., (1946–48); Carmen Gómez Tejera and David Cruz López, *La escuela puertorriqueña* (Sharon, Conn: Troutman Press, 1970); and Cayetano Coll y Toste, *Historia de la instrucción en Puerto Rico hasta el año 1898* (San Juan: El Boletín Mercantil, 1910).

2.   Gómez Tejera and Cruz López, op. cit., 51.

3.   Luis M. Díaz Soler, *La esclavitud negra en Puerto Rico* (San Juan: Editorial Universitaria, 1967).

4.   María Luisa de Angelis, *Mujeres puertorriqueñas* (San Juan: El Boletín Mercantil, 1908), 6.

5.   Ibid, 8.

6.   Josefina Rivera de Alvarez, *Diccionario de la Literatura Puertorriqueña, Tomo 2, Volumen 1*, (San Juan de Puerto Rico: Instituto de Cultura Puertorriqueña, 1974). A new edition of *Aguinaldo Puertorriqueño*, was published by Terranova Editores, San Juan, Puerto Rico in 2004..

7.   Cuesta Mendoza, op.cit.

8.   Ibid, 85.

9.   Ibid.

10. Ibid.

11. Juan José Osuna, *A History of Education in Puerto Rico* (Río Piedras: Editorial Universitaria, 1949).

12. Cuesta Mendoza, op. cit., 39–42.

13. *Reglamento de la Asociación de Damas para la Instrucción de la Mujer* (San Juan: El Boletín Mercantil, 1886).

14. Lidio Cruz Monclova, *Historia de Puerto Rico, Siglo XIX* (Río Piedras: Editorial Universitaria, 1971) 728–729.

15. Lidio Cruz Monclova, "El movimiento de las ideas en el Puerto Rico del siglo XIX," Boletín de la Academia Puertorriqueña de la Lengua Española, II. 3–4 (1974): 81–100.

16. See: "Olympe de Gouges, Feminist and Revolutionary Republican," in *Women as Revolutionary*, ed. Frederick G. Griffin (New York: Mentor, 1973), 46–49. The Manifesto written by Olympe de Gouges entitled *The Declaration of Women's Rights and Citizenship* revolutionized the discussion on the status of women, advancing the libertarian process.

17. One of the cornerstones in the development of feminist theory is *Vindication of the Rights of Woman* by Mary Wollstonecraft (1792). Wollstonecraft shared her life with William Godwin, one of the forerunners of anarchist thought, who influenced her as much as she influenced him.

18. With regard to this subject I recommend the extensive article by Juliet Mitchell, "Women: The Longest Revolution," *New Left Review*, no. 40, 1966. Also the seminal texts, *Economic and Philosophic Manuscripts* by Karl Marx, and *The Origin of the Family* by Frederick Engels.

19. There are several serious documents that record the development of feminism to the present. I recommend the works of English writer Sheila Rowbotham,

Women's Consciousness, Man's World and *Women, Resistance and Revolution*, also a short essay by Magda Oranich, *¿Qué es feminismo?* (Barcelona: Editorial La Gaya Ciencia, 1976).

20. *Reglamento*, op. cit., 2. See Appendix A for the complete text.

21. Cuesta Mendoza, op.cit., 235.

22. Manuel Fernández Juncos, "Prólogo" in *La mujer en Puerto Rico*, Gabriel Ferrer Hernández (San Juan: Imprenta El Agenta, 1881), xii.

23. Alejandro Tapia y Rivera, *El Bardo de Guamaní* (La Habana: Imprenta del Tiempo, 1883), 590.

24. Eugenio María de Hostos, "Forjando el porvenir americano," in *Obras Completas, Vol. I* (San Juan: Instituto de Cultura Puertorriqueña, 1969), 8–9.

25. Josefina Moll, "La Mujer" in *Mujeres Puertorriqueñas*, de Angelis, 120.

26. María Luisa de Angelis as well as Ana Roqué de Duprey published numerous books and edited newspapers, among them, *Pluma de Mujer* by de Angelis and *El Heraldo de la Mujer* by Roqué.

27. See Gervasio García "Primeros fermentos de organización obrera en Puerto Rico, 1873–1898" in *Desafío y solidaridad, breve historia del movimiento obrero puertorriqueño* (Río Piedras: Ediciones Huracán, 1982).

28. Emphasis in the original. *Third Philosophical Manuscript in Economic and Philosophic Manuscripts of 1844* by Karl Marx (New York: International Publishers,1964).

29. The following are among the anarchist texts consulted: Irving L. Horowitz, *The Anarchists* (New York: Dell Publishing Company, 1964); George Woodstock, *Anarchism, a History of Libertarian Ideas and Movements* (Chicago: Meridian, 1962); Roderick Kedward, *The Anarchists—The Men Who Shocked an Era* (New York: American Heritage Press, 1971); and Federica Montseny, *¿Qué es anarquismo?* (Barcelona: Editorial La Gaya Ciencia, 1976).

30. Selected anarchist books by Puerto Rican workers are: Venancio Cruz, *Hacia el porvenir* (San Juan: Tipografía La República Española, n.d.); Angel María Dieppa, *El porvenir social* (Puerta de Tierra: Tipografía El Eco, 1915); and Alfonso Torres, *Solidaridad* (San Juan de Puerto Rico: Union Tipográfica, 1905).

31. García, op. cit.

CHAPTER II

The Making of a Feminist

Luisa Capetillo was born on October 28, 1879, in the town of Arecibo on the island of Puerto Rico, the "natural" or illegitimate child of Margarita Perón and Luis Capetillo Echevarría.[1] Luisa Margarita Perone, who later hispanicized her last name to Perón, was a native of France and a French citizen.[2] She arrived in Puerto Rico at a very young age as the governess of the Zeno family of Arecibo.[3] By 1874, when she was 26 years old, she was still living in Arecibo, single, and working as a domestic.[4] Luis Capetillo Echevarría arrived in Puerto Rico around the same time as Margarita, traveling with his family from the Basque country of Spain. His father was Luis Capetillo Ruz, and his mother Magdalena Echevarría. Their children were Luis, Antonio and Rafaela. The family, who claimed to be descendents of the French "Capetos," established themselves in the Caribbean island with enough financial means to live comfortably, if not affluently. The sons soon became independent, starting their own families, while Rafaela remained at home, living with her parents in Santurce.

The young men arrived from Northern Spain full of advanced ideas about citizens' and workers' rights and ideas that were circulating throughout their native province near France. Antonio married Isidora García Restos and had a large family. Luis, on the other hand, became involved in a relationship with the Frenchwoman Margarita Perón, without any legally binding ties. The couple established their residence in Arecibo where Luisa, their only daughter, was born. She was reared with great love while her intellectual capacity was carefully and conscientiously developed.

Luisa Capetillo, and later her own children, maintained a close relationship with Luis's single sister Rafaela, who inherited her parents' fortune and lived to an old age on Dos Hermanos Street in Santurce.[5] Luis and his brother Antonio, along with Antonio's children, have continued to this day to question the whereabouts of the Capetillo fortune which passed from Rafaela's hands to her relative and executor don Pablo Ubarri, Count of Santurce.[6] Luisa Capetillo never made any claims to the fortune that may in part have belonged to her, and consequently lived a life of sacrifice and struggle in the service of the oppressed.

Luis Capetillo and Margarita Perón shared several characteristics when they joined their lives. Both had been ideologically influenced in Europe in the aftermath of the French Revolution. Margarita lived during the time of revolutionary Romanticism that had its beginnings in the Revolution of 1848, and which primarily mobilized women to defend their ideas and behave in new ways. The writer George Sand, considered a liberated woman for her time, personified the prototype of the "new woman," revolutionary, both politically and in her personal life, opposed to marriage and to all social contracts that would regulate human relations, but willing to sacrifice everything in the name of love. The heroines of her pastoral novels lived the ecstasy of Romanticism, but at the same time supported the liberation of workers and slaves.[7]

The work of George Sand spread throughout nineteenth century Europe, as did the stories about her personal life. The French novelist put into practice the ideas she espoused in theory, at times influencing European women more by her lifestyle than by her literary work. In France as well as in England and Germany the frenzy caused by Sand's ideas quickly took hold. Well known English historian Edward Hallett Carr's work about the famous "Romantic exiles" (Russian anarchists Bakunin, Herzen, and Ogarev), detailed the echoes of Romanticism and the French Revolution and how they resonated throughout Europe. These ideas ultimately evolved into a naturalist and human liberation movement that greatly influenced the development of anarchist theories.

Carr noted, "A movement existed in Europe that favored the cult to nature and the liberation of the individual from the yoke of moral and political absolutism...In its first and most characteristic phase, it was not a movement against religion and morality per se. Those who attacked conventional morality did not claim to deny the existence of moral sanctions. The cult to human nature filled the void and resulted in the establishment of moral codes like Rousseau's, based on the primacy of feelings, or like George Sand's, on the religion of love."[8] Margarita Perón, like her daughter Luisa later on, followed the beliefs of Sand and made Sand's cult to love and nature her own. In fact, during her lifetime, Luisa Capetillo was often compared to George Sand. Carr

added, "If the author of the romantic creed was Rousseau, its popular-
izer and vulgarizer was George Sand. The modern reader only sees her
as a naïve woman and an ultra sentimental narrator of stories not lively
enough to be read as a distraction, nor solid enough to gain respect
for its author as one would respect the author of a classic. Nevertheless, Europe of the nineteenth century, especially 'Female Europe,' con-
sistently practiced and advocated the development of Rousseaunian
doctrine whose general principles had already been elaborated by the
formidable Madame Stael."[9]

In Russia, the cradle of anarchist theoreticians, Romanticism and
the prototype of the "new woman" came about later because of different social conditions. But it also caught fire like an inextinguishable
flame, to the point of driving some women to romantic paroxysms.
Natalia Herzen, wife of anarchist-philosopher Alexander Herzen, expressed her devotion to the French writer in a letter, "Oh great Sand!
How deeply has this woman touched human nature! How daringly has
she guided the living soul through sin and libertinism, only to extract
it unharmed from the flame that devours all!"[10] Romanticism came to
America even later, but also caught fire with that same fervor that not
only inspired different behavior, but also an exalted and passionate literary style. In Puerto Rico, literary historians trace the development of
Romanticism to the first decade of the 1900s.

Luisa Capetillo's mother, Margarita Perón, was born in Romantic
France, grew up with its influence, and arrived in the Caribbean with
her ideas and cultivated them there, as she influenced those who were
close to her, primarily her daughter, who also became a child of Romanticism.[11] Margarita Perón lived like one of Sand's heroines, joined
without legal ties to the man she loved, working to support herself,
and imbuing her daughter Luisa with a sense of freedom. Luisa would
later dedicate revealing words to her mother, saying that she had fostered her free, uncensored thinking and had supported her when she
decided to challenge the established order with her ideas and behavior,
"To you, dear mother of mine, who never tried to control me, or make
me think traditionally. You allowed me to inquire freely, only reproach-
ing what you thought were exaggerations, without forcing me in any
way."[12]

Her father, Luis Capetillo, came from Northern Spain, where the
movement for workers' rights was growing in importance, and anarchistic ideas were stirring the *campesinos*, later paving the way for
the creation of some of the first libertarian nuclei in Spain.[13] Margarita
Perón and Luis Capetillo shared other traits. Both came to Puerto Rico

to make their fortune, and at first found jobs of some social prestige—she as a governess, and he as the impresario and administrator of a kind of amusement park, a concept brought from Europe. However, as they were forced by economic circumstances to accept proletarian employment, they lost status within conservative Puerto Rican society. Luis began to work on the docks, in construction or agriculture, depending on the season of the year and the availability of jobs. Meanwhile, in family gatherings or at the café, he continually referred to himself as a count working as a laborer.[14]

Margarita Perón was forced to work as a laundrywoman and a presser in the homes of wealthy families in town. But she never abandoned the European custom of attending the afternoon gatherings at the café. Every afternoon, well into the first decade of the twentieth century, she attended the *tertulia* (traditional gatherings in which men would meet over coffee and discuss various topics of interest), at her friend don Nicasio Sánchez's *Cafetín Misisipí*. She was the only woman at these tertulias. She was considered a "different kind of woman," with advanced ideas from "over there," referring to Europe. "*La Francesa*" (The Frenchwoman), as she was called, was described by those who knew her as "chubby, short, very fair-skinned, grey-haired and very sweet." She also practiced French with the youngsters from the high school in Arecibo.[15]

Luis and Margarita provided their daughter with a carefully designed education, something not very common among Puerto Rican women at that time, despite the efforts of the liberals to secure greater access to education for women. Capetillo's formal schooling faithfully reflected the state of women's education in Puerto Rico. However, her private education at home made her upbringing totally different from the majority of the women of her time. Her father taught her to read and write, and instructed her in the basic rules of arithmetic. Later she attended the private school of Doña María Sierra Soler where she was awarded various diplomas for her achievements in grammar, religious history, geography, and reading.[16]

Where Luisa Capetillo truly acquired her vast culture was through the independent reading that she did during her lifetime, beginning in childhood. She read the works of the French writers, Victor Hugo and Emile Zola, the Russian Romantics, Leo Tolstoy and Turgenev, and the French astronomer, spiritualist and freethinker Camille Flammarion, whose research on astronomy and psychical studies she avidly read. Her own work reflects the ease with which she handled the theories and texts of influential authors such as the French doctor Paul Vigne, of

Hugo and Tolstoy, the writings of anarchist educator Madeleine Vernet, and the philosophical-political essays of Peter Kropotkin and John Stuart Mill.

Once, while noticing a wrinkle in a blank piece of paper, she reasoned, "What is deformed...can be special," and "Nothing should be looked down upon, nor elevated among other things. At times a human deformity is necessary and inspires notable reflections and produces beautiful things."[17] Capetillo asserted that people can stop the waters and enrich the rivers, but nature is nature and will always prevail. She believed the essence of nature would always be present in a "natural" deformity, as well as in something beautiful that is also natural. Capetillo took advantage of the incident of the wrinkled paper to reflect upon Quasimodo, the famous fictional character created by Victor Hugo in *The Hunchback of Notre Dame*. Bearing in mind the literary metaphor of the French writer, she was inspired to put into writing her own ideas about life and nature, obligatory topics for anarchists, who believed in the natural state of man and woman. A common theme of nineteenth century Romanticism, as Irving L. Horowitz described in *The Anarchists,* is the belief that "the closer behavior is to being natural, the closer it will be to a just society. The anarchists, along with the utopians, will try to test this branch of Romanticism."[18] Through her ideas and behavior Luisa Capetillo reflected her mother's influence as much as the influence of her own anarchist and romantic readings.

On June 24, 1890, at the age of eleven, Luisa Capetillo was taken by her mother to be baptized in the church of San Felipe Apóstol in Arecibo. Her godparents were the mayor of the town, don Policarpo Echevarría, and his wife doña María Asunción Echevarría. The priest, Lucas Lladó, celebrated the Catholic sacrament of baptism, and don Bernardo Blaudino acted as godfather, in the mayor's stead, since he did not attend the baptism. It is not known whether Margarita Perón was a personal friend of the mayor, which could have resulted in a relationship of *compadrazgo* (godparenthood), so important in Puerto Rico. In the nineteenth century it was a common practice for the mayor to be godfather to a large number of children from different social classes.

Even though she was baptized as a child, Luisa Capetillo was not a practicing Catholic as an adult. On the contrary, she was virulently anticlerical, repudiating Catholicism and its representatives—the priests—whom she accused of being hypocrites. In her *Ensayos libertarios* (Libertarian Essays), she exhorts, "*Compañeros,* don't baptize your children. Think about it. If it were so necessary, it would be stupid for there to be millions of human beings who don't believe in it."[19] She never baptized her children and in heartfelt words to Manuela she explained, "I never taught you to pray, that is something you have to feel. You are not baptized by any religious rite."[20] Her opinion was that baptism enslaved human beings. She protested against that "denigrating mark by not taking any children to the contaminated baptismal font because I was no slave."[21]

Luisa Capetillo believed that human beings should not be slaves to rituals or dogmas. Since the Catholic religion depends on both, she felt it should be repudiated. She referred to priests as "the ones with black robes," and considered them hypocrites, mainly interested in upholding the traditional system, which perpetuated the exploitation of workers while the rich bourgeoisie became richer. In her opinion, priests promoted obscurantism so that women and men, without thinking or analyzing, came to believe in dogmas, making education unnecessary and promoting ignorance and the status quo. Furthermore, Capetillo believed that religious ceremonies such as the Mass were traditionally used by bourgeois women to show off their fancy dresses and jewelry. She viewed it as a system based on envy, idleness and social inequality.[22]

Nevertheless, Luisa Capetillo, in contrast to the majority of the anarchist-theorists who defended atheism, believed in a true Christianity that perhaps can be defined as individual and voluntary. Capetillo easily responded to those who criticized her for being both an anarchist and a Christian, a faithful believer in the immortality of the soul and also in the spiritual world. In her essay, "*¿Anarquista y Espiritista?...¡Uf, Uf!*" (Anarchist and Spiritist?...Humph!), Capetillo defended the concept of deity as wisdom or "perfect knowledge" of the origin of the world, and explained that there was no contradiction between spiritism and anarchism, and that humans, with their pettiness, created contradictions where there were none. She asserted:

> I don't see why the scientific concept of Spiritism should be opposed to that of Anarchy. The direction of both is a matter of more or less passionate temperaments. If we were to take Spiritism along the path of violence, it would lose its superiority as a philosophical concept. Anarchy doesn't promote violence either. Anarchy states that no one has the right to govern or exploit another, or to monopolize the land or tools of labor. It also states that no individual should hold a job that goes against his or her aspirations, preferences or convenience. Nor should any two people who are repulsive to each other be forced to cohabitate. They should be free to be together or apart. Which of the anarchist objectives does Spiritism reject? [23]

In this way Capetillo eloquently rationalized the fact that in her daily life she practiced both philosophies: anarchism and spiritism. By day she would give a talk about anarchism to a group of workers, and on the same night, address a spiritist group.

She attempted to transmit to her children her concept of religion and Christianity. In a letter she asked her daughter Manuela to be a good Christian but without submitting to the strict rules of a particular church, for example, the Catholic Church. She urged her to find her own ways of following the Christian maxims. She told her, "The only thing I want and hope from you is that you are a good human being, not a Christian by rote. You can be an interpreter of the maxims of Jesus without attending Mass, without going to confession, receiving communion, or accepting any kind of dogma of lies from an organized religion."[24] She advised her that instead of attending Mass and following archaic rituals, she should visit the poor, the prisoners and the sick. She should believe in justice and equality, support the liberation of both workers and women, get rid of superfluous luxuries, and be "natural," practicing honesty and charity. For Luisa Capetillo, to be a Christian was to preach the total eradication of the exploitation of one group of human beings by another, and to believe sincerely that all human beings are equal. Her philosophy and her way of life were close to the preachings and practices of Tolstoy, whose books she avidly read, recommending them to her readers and listeners.

An intellectual aristocrat who lived the life of a wealthy feudal lord, Tolstoy wrote his major literary works mainly during his youth and early adulthood. In 1870 he experienced a spiritual crisis that caused him to reevaluate his previous beliefs. From that point on, as explained by Irving L. Horowitz, he defended a rationalistic branch of Evangelical Christianity based on a fundamental principle of fraternal love and passive resistance to evil. The achievement of inner freedom and personal rectitude through this doctrine caused him to look for the social applications it could have. He rejected the established Church as a corruptor of the maxims of Christ and he opposed the State, since it was based on the use of force. Tolstoy became an ascetic, repudiating the property he inherited from his family and living the life of a farmer, sharing their simplicity and their poverty. Tolstoy asserted, in what were considered later, his anarchist papers, "Property is the root of all evil."[25] Consequently, the rich should give up their belongings because, "Once the temptation to justify the power of money disappears, the desire to exploit others will also disappear."[26]

The world view that Tolstoy embraced in his later years was of spiritual peace and physical asceticism, of harmony between the aristocrat-turned-farmer and the servants who served him with care and devotion, even after he rejected their submission. His anarchist writings reflected this ideal world, and his recommendations, both to the rich and the working class, can be considered idealistic, perhaps even utopian. His analysis of society lacked a detailed study of the economy of power, and although feasible in his own circumstances, was impractical for the rest of society.

Capetillo, however, found inspiration in his teachings, as she developed her own opinion of what Christianity should be, and thought they should be practiced by everyone. Tolstoy believed that redemption would come through harmonious coexistence of the rich, who would renounce their property, and the peasants, who worked the land. Capetillo believed that redemption would result from the organization and liberation of the workers, who would rid themselves of the bosses and landlords, all of whom were "bourgeois exploiters" because their religious beliefs were insincere and hypocritical. Harmonious coexistence among the social classes, a common idea to both Capetillo and Tolstoy, would survive without any government or church, in a state of perfect communism. Capetillo expected the bosses, landlords and rich bourgeoisie to be transformed like Tolstoy, through reasoning. Convinced of their past errors, they would happily give up their possessions, becoming true Christians. Like all good anarchists, Capetillo not only adopted Tolstoy's philosophy, but also his lifestyle as her example and inspiration.

The play that she wrote in 1909, *Influencias de las ideas modernas* (The Influence of Modern Ideas), published in San Juan in 1916, was inspired by Tolstoy's philosophy and included a main character who resembled him. In don Juan de Ramírez, we find the wealthy bourgeois—owner of a factory in Arecibo—whose conscience is awakened by his daughter Angelina, an autobiographical character based on Capetillo. The direction of the play is established from the beginning of the first act when Angelina appears, reading Tolstoy's book *Modern Slavery*. Through this and other anarchist books, Angelina comes to understand that the laborers and the farmers, because they are closer to nature and less tainted by Western civilization, are the ones who act with truth and justice. When she is reminded that it's her birthday and many greeting cards and expensive gifts have arrived for her, Angelina says, "Actually, I didn't remember, I've been so distracted lately reading this book by Tolstoy, *Modern Slavery*, which has convinced me that modern slavery is the iron law of wages."[27] Later on, Angelina explains to the leaders of the workers why she believes and preaches the "anarchist maxims."

She says, "Well, my friends, don't let my ways surprise you. I have read Malatesta, Tolstoy and Zola, so I have understood many things that I couldn't before."[28]

Don Juan de Ramírez, like Tolstoy, is convinced through instruction, education, and without violence, that he must give up his possessions to the community and transform his lifestyle into a more "natural" and fair one. Don Juan and his daughter Angelina join the workers in "solidarity" and together go to work in the cooperatives. Having rejected luxury and privilege, the bourgeoisie who arrive at the workers community are greeted by them with cheers for "the new woman," who now can and will live in freedom. They shout "Long live the free woman! Praise to the woman who rejected all privilege and tradition and is helping us to achieve freedom!"[29] Tolstoy's lasting impression upon Capetillo is evident in this drama.

Capetillo spent her formative teenage years reading romantic European literature. However, even with this unique intellectual background, she was essentially just a young girl from Arecibo, daughter of a presser. Luisa would go with her mother to the homes of wealthy Puerto Ricans that her mother worked for. At the residence of don Gregorio Ledesma, the leader of the *Partido Incondicional Español* (Pro-Spain Party) and Marquis of Arecibo, she met his son Manuel Ledesma, who fell in love with her. Manuel and his close friend, Dr. Susoni, competed for the love of "the daughter of the French lady," as she was called, with Ledesma the victor, winning the heart of the young Luisa. Years later, the quarrel between the two friends continued, ending in a duel, provoked by the young Marquis' jealousy.

Around 1897, Manuel Ledesma, heir to his father's fortune and aristocratic title, single and still living in his parents' home, took Luisa as his lover. By then her own father was not present in her life, and no further mention of him has been recorded. In 1898, while Puerto Rico was being invaded by United States troops led by General Miles and the Island was handed over to the United States as part of its spoils of war, Capetillo was giving birth to her first born, Manuela. Two years later, when Capetillo was only twenty, her second child Gregorio was born. The young mother and her two children lived with Margarita Perón until the lovers separated and Luisa joined the salaried labor force.

Luisa Capetillo loved Manuel Ledesma and the children from that union. She wrote emotionally about him in the essay "*A ti*" (To You), included in her book *Mi opinión*. She lyrically described her love and the anguish she suffered due to this illicit relationship, including the condemnation by the young Marquis' family and all of Arecibo. Although no legal contract bound them, they had a traditional union, based on her inferior status as a female in submission to the male. She had no rights in this relationship since she could not demand her lover's company or his moral or economic support, and yet she had the responsibility of raising and educating their children. However, her deepest resentment was the absolute fidelity he demanded of her, making her stay cloistered in her home, exclusively performing the duties of a mother and housewife, while he enjoyed his own freedom. Capetillo told Manuel Ledesma in her memoirs:

> And now, painful tears fall when I remember that loving uneasiness that came from my ignorance about the struggles of life, human lies and betrayals...Remembering the one I waited for on endless nights, with an unbelievable loneliness that I wrapped myself in so I could feel comfortable...thinking and waiting to hear the sound of the small bronze door knocker that would end my eternal longing, a longing that destroyed my illusions and cruelly humiliated me: the desire to have the master of my thoughts and feelings by my side, the one who made life blossom in me, duplicating itself in two beings, fruit of my spontaneous love, without trammels or subterfuge, without hypocrisy or self interest...only tarnished by one detail...a woman, a mother, who symbolized for me all social norms.[30]

While she suffered deeply from the loss of her ideal love, Capetillo used her experiences with the Marquis of Arecibo to define and develop her feminist philosophy. Though the Ledesma-Capetillo relationship lasted more than three years, historical facts about the immediate causes for their separation are elusive. Was it pressure from the young man's family for him to marry a woman from his social class, pressure from social conventions, or Capetillo's own desperation, seeing herself as condemned to a hermetic life? In truth, it appears that Capetillo thoroughly lived the Romantic ideal in this relationship, romanticizing and idealizing both the image of the loved one and his indifference. Capetillo "trembled," a classic effect of Romanticism, as she contemplated her misfortune, just as George Sand's heroines used to do. The heroine of Sand's novel, *Jaques*, exclaimed in one of the passages, "Why would it be a sin to abandon myself to my heart? It is when one can no longer love that one should cry for oneself and be ashamed for allowing the sacred flame to be extinguished." E.H. Carr further described the romantic personality when he observed, "The new woman would blush, not when she loved, but when she couldn't find a lover."[31] Luisa Capetillo didn't regret having loved, but rather regretted not having lived more freely. Even so, she turned her love for Ledesma into a platonic one that lasted for years after their relationship was over.

Manuel Ledesma, who later became the mayor of Arecibo, legally recognized his children and took care of their education. He also provided economic support for Luisa's mother, who cared for their children so that Luisa could dedicate herself to her job as a union organizer and reader in the tobacco factories. Capetillo made continuous references to the relationship she had with her children. She read her works to them and told them stories about her trips throughout the Island and abroad.

Life for the Ledesma-Capetillo children, however, was conflictive. Her daughter, Manuela, was enrolled by her father in the Catholic boarding school *La Inmaculada* in Manatí. There the nuns vehemently condemned the letters that her mother sent her, and would hand her mere scraps of paper after they had censored what they considered obscene. One of the "obscenities" was Luisa's recommendation that Manuela shower naked every day, not weekly, and without a tunic covering her body, a procedure established by the school. When Manuela, while still very young, got married, her husband forbade her to receive her mother in their home, since he thought Luisa was too radical and considered her influence dangerous.

Her son Gregorio was a constant source of worry for Luisa, who sent him socks, underwear and heartfelt advice from New York, where she traveled on various occasions as part of her job as a journalist and union organizer. A letter sent to him by don Manuel Ledesma from Arecibo in 1921 reflects family disagreements and paternal reprimands. "I hope this time you won't lie to me like you did before. It reflects a lack of seriousness unseemly for a person of good birth."[32] His father ended by sending him his love, but not without first reminding him that he should be honest at all times. Family continued to be important to Gregorio and Manuela. They maintained a relationship with their father's family, and also kept in touch with their aunts, uncles and cousins on their mother's side.

Capetillo considered maternity one of the most beautiful functions nature reserved for women. After she gave birth she declared, "I feel I would not be a complete woman if I weren't a mother. A complete woman should be a mother."[33] She believed, however, that due to the nature of woman, "...a woman will always be a mother, even if she doesn't have children."[34] Capetillo had a constant concern for children, both her own and poor, destitute children without homes. The education of future generations also occupied her thoughts and writings.

Luisa Capetillo's parents, her environment, personal experiences, and her readings of the European Romantics and revolutionaries, were the axis around which her personality was shaped. Gradually, she became a proponent of the movement for the emancipation of workers and women in Puerto Rico, a movement in which she herself would emerge as a leader.

NOTES

1. Baptismal records from the Catedral San Felipe Apóstol, Arecibo, Book 40, page 57.
2. Estela Sifre de Loubriel, *Catálogo de extranjeros residentes en Puerto Rico en Siglo XIX* (San Juan: Instituto de Cultura Puertorriqueña, Lista de Francia, #872), 70.
3. Testimony of Manuela Ledesma Capetillo. Taped personal interview, 1974.
4. Sifre de Loubriel, loc. cit.
5. Testimony of Julie Capetillo de Fair, Luisa Capetillo's niece, who supported this project from its early stages. Taped personal interview, 1976.
6. Ibid.
7. See Silvina Bullrich, *Una mujer como yo* (Buenos Aires: Emecé, 1946) as well as George Sand's pastoral novels, *Indiana* and *La Petite Fadette*.
8. E.H. Carr, *The Romantic Exiles*, (London, 1933).
9. Ibid., 58.
10. Ibid., 59.
11. Josefina Rivera de Alvarez, "Romanticismo", in *Diccionario de la literatura puertorriqueña, Vol. I* (San Juan: Instituto de Cultura Puertorriqueña, 1974).
12. Luisa Capetillo, *Mi opinión* (San Juan: Biblioteca Roja, 1911), unpaginated.
13. See Santiago Iglesias Pantín, *Luchas emancipadoras*, an autobiographical work that describes his anarchist roots in the North of Spain.
14. Testimony of José Rosa, Luisa Capetillo's son-in-law for fifteen years. Taped personal interview, 1974.
15. Testimony of Nabal Barreto, participant with Margarita Perón at the literary and political salons they attended in Arecibo. Taped personal interview, 1976.
16. Luisa Capetillo, *Influencias de las ideas modernas* (San Juan: Tipografía Negrón Flores, 1916), 74.
17. Capetillo, *Mi opinión*, 140.
18. Irving L. Horowitz, *Los Anarquistas* (Madrid: Alianza Editorial, 1964), 63. (*The Anarchists*, New York: Dell Publishing, 1964).
19. Luisa Capetillo, *Ensayos libertarios* (San Juan: Tipografía Real Hermanos, 1909), 19.
20. Capetillo, *Mi opinión*, 83.
21. Capetillo, *Influencias*, 79.
22. Capetillo, *Ensayos*, 23-24.
23. Capetillo, *Mi opinión*, Second Edition, 170-171.

24.   Ibid., 81.
25.   Horowitz, op. cit., 274.
26.   Ibid., 285.
27.   Capetillo, *Influencias*, 6.
28.   Ibid., 32. Capetillo refers to the theoreticians of anarchism, Carlos Malato, Errico Malatesta and Leo Tolstoy; the novels of Emile Zola were also read by Romantic anarchists like herself.
29.   Ibid., 48.
30.   Capetillo, *Mi opinión*, 188.
31.   E.H. Carr, op. cit., 58.
32.   Typewritten letter, part of the author's collection.
33.   Capetillo, *Influencias*, 65.
34.   Ibid., 86.

Fig. 4. Manuelita and Gregorio Ledesma Capetillo, children of Luisa Capetillo and Manuel
Ledesma, c. 1905.

CHAPTER III

Life as a Moral Drama

At the beginning of the twentieth century Luisa Capetillo began writing for the newspaper of her native city, Arecibo, while she was developing her political ideas based on the theories of libertarian socialism. Her principal ideological source was the work of the Romantic anarchists, and in practice, through her daily struggles with her fellow workers, she came to define her own revolutionary ideas.

Her relationship with landowner Manuel Ledesma dissolved when Capetillo joined the ranks of the wage earners who worked at home, embroidering and stitching handkerchiefs and blouses that were later picked up by a middleman who sold them to United States investors. She did not earn much and although she thought it was Ledesma's duty to support her, she preferred not to accept his money. She said of Ledesma in her memoirs, "I have made a living from my work for a long time; perhaps he believed he had the responsibility to support me, and he really did. That didn't bother me, but I wanted to prove that I could support myself, producing something without nonsense or exaggeration."[1]

She became a reader in the Arecibo tobacco factories where she deepened her knowledge of the culture and political ideas of the oppressed, specifically Puerto Ricans. Her job was to continuously read aloud to the workers. She read Puerto Rican and foreign newspapers, novels by Victor Hugo, "the poet of the oppressed," the works of Balzac, Flaubert, Dumas, Dostoyevsky and Tolstoy, as well as works on political theory. Along with European thinkers and writers, she included several from the Americas. José María Vargas Vila, Colombian journalist and novelist, whose radical political ideas resonated with the workers, was also a favorite of Capetillo and her audience. The readers were paid by the workers, who took up collections among themselves, or by contributions from the factory owners, if the union won this privilege through collective bargaining.[2] The reader was seated on a raised platform, called *la tribuna*, and read with a loud and clear voice so that the strippers, who removed veins and stems from tobacco leaves, and those who manufactured the cigars, could listen. It was a tradition among the workers to hit the table with their working tools if they wanted the reader to repeat a passage over and over, indefinitely. In this way the tobacco workers, even if they were illiterate, were exposed to a vast political culture, sometimes memorizing extensive passages from literary works. It became a tradition among them to stop and discuss complicated chapters and political theory. "Readers commanded an almost reverential respect," according to Mormino and Pozzeta, professors who studied the labor world of Ybor City. [3] They quote Cuban national leader and writer José Martí as saying that "the readers' platforms in the factories were advanced pulpits of liberty." *

These ideas—some progressive and others truly revolutionary—reached the enlightened Puerto Rican workers in this way. Newspapers, pamphlets and books, mainly from Madrid, Havana, New York and Buenos Aires, were important sources of literature, current events and new ideas. During the last decades of the nineteenth century, books such as *Federalism and Socialism* by Bakunin, the seminal theoretical work about anarcho-unionism, and other books of equal importance were published in Puerto Rico. In study groups, the most progressive workers, especially the craftsmen, typographers, and tobacco workers, regularly discussed *The Conquest of Bread: Fields, Factories and Workshops* by the anarchist collectivist Piotr Kropotkin, *Anarchy* by Errico Malatesta, *Moribund Society and Anarchy* by Jean Grave and other anarchist texts relating to the theme of society in the future.[4]

Study groups which met frequently in organized meetings offered workers the opportunity to discuss various theoretical treatises designed to raise the workers' consciousness and put into practice the theory of labor organization. Newspapers from various countries, *Porvenir del Trabajo* (The Future of Work), *La Revista Blanca* (The White Magazine), *El Socialismo* (Socialism) and the well known Cuban anarchistic newspaper *Tierra* (Land), arrived on the Island in different ways, mainly as contraband through workers who came from Cuba, Panama and the Dominican Republic. These study groups deeply influenced the workers who eventually made a name for themselves during the first three decades of the twentieth century, a decisive period in the de-

---

*Translator's Note. It is interesting to note that the 2003 Pulitzer Prize-winning play, *Anna in the Tropics* by Cuban-American Nilo Cruz, is about a factory reader and how his choice to read the novel *Anna Karenina* affects the lives of the workers.

velopment of the Puerto Rican labor movement. Santiago Iglesias Pantín, José Ferrer y Ferrer, Alonso Torres and Ramón Romero Rosa were actively involved as leaders who participated in the workers' struggle on the Island from the beginning. Luisa Capetillo distinguished herself along with them.

Through her work as a reader, Luisa Capetillo was in contact with the leaders of the labor movement, especially those affiliated with the *Federación de Torcedores de Tabaco* (Federation of Tobacco Rollers). This group was allied with the *Federación Libre de Trabajadores de Puerto Rico* (Free Libertarian Federation of Puerto Rican Workers), a group founded in 1902 that maintained close contact with tobacco workers in Florida, Panama, the Dominican Republic and Cuba.

Capetillo made her "debut" as a labor organizer in Arecibo in 1905, at an agricultural workers' strike that covered the entire northern region of the country. This strike was led by the *Federación Libre de Trabajadores* of Arecibo.[5] Commenting on her role as a union leader, Capetillo noted that she did it on her own, unguided and alone. She stated, "...I have presented myself as an activist, a journalist, and a writer without any permission other than my own calling and initiative, without any encouragement and with no help other than my own will."[6] Her pro-union collaboration with Arecibo newspapers paved the way for her to assume a leadership role during the agricultural workers' strike. It was during the crucible of this experience that she began her long and successful work as an activist and a labor organizer. Journalist Santiago Carreras described the historic moment and Capetillo's passion as he recalled, "Luisa Capetillo at the head of the march, along with other leaders, haranguing the workers...her great mission was to read aloud to them, which she did, atop benches of the plaza."[7]

Her role in the Arecibo strike determined the direction of her life. There Luisa Capetillo became a union leader, from that moment on dedicating herself, with equal success, to organizing workers and to spreading anarcho-syndical ideas through her writings in pamphlets and newspaper articles, in talks, rallies, lectures and private gatherings. She constantly traveled throughout the Island by train, meeting with groups of workers, sharing directives from the FLT's leadership, and selling newspapers and magazines, which allowed her to support herself. In the FLT's newspaper, *Unión Obrera* (Workers Union), notes continually appeared announcing Capetillo's visit to a particular town and informing the public that she would be selling her pamphlets as well as the newspapers, *Unión Obrera* and *Motín* (Strike) from Madrid or *Tierra* from Havana.

In 1907 she published her first book, *Ensayos libertarios* (Libertarian Essays). Written from November 1904 to November 1907, it contains her ideas about an egalitarian and just society in which Puerto Rican workers of both sexes enjoy the rights that are denied to them by their bosses, whom she considers tyrants and exploiters. Just like the classic anarchists, Bakunin, Malatesta, Sorel and Kropotkin, her acknowledged teachers, she conceives of anarchism as a "way of life" rather than a "vision of the future." What anarchism offers, according to political scientist Irving L. Horowitz, is a belief in "natural man," as more essential and historically preceding "political man." Capetillo also believed that human beings, left in their natural state, but educated in search of truth, will always be kind, egalitarian and consequently, Christian. They will return to the truth, stripped of rites and dogma, and in practicing brotherhood they will find the basis of happiness in their fellowman. Capetillo preached love for her fellowman. For her, "fellowman" meant the women, the poor, the workers, the laborers and their families, because the capitalists and landowners were sinners, evil people, who would need to give up their possessions to the community in order to save themselves and find true happiness. Deprived of all material wealth, they too could enjoy a natural life. As we saw in the previous chapter, the true representation of this philosophy was Leo Tolstoy.

As Horowitz brilliantly asserts, the anarchist image of life takes on the characteristics of a moral drama in which individuals fight with fervent religious zeal against existing social systems. This drama defined the very essence of Capetillo's life and work. For her, work is good and leisure is bad; the poor are noble and the rich are sinners. Because of their nature, all human beings are equal, although socially they are stratified. Capetillo deplored the misery that the Puerto Rican workers and *campesinos* lived in. She was clearly moved when she described how they labor from dawn to dusk for a few miserable cents, victims of malaria, tuberculosis and exhaustion. She suffered for the needy children who lived without intellectual or physical sustenance. She accused judges and condemned the landowners and capitalist bosses of causing all the misfortunes perpetuated upon so many thousands of human beings. She called them "parasites," "mollusks stuck to rocks," and demanded that those rocks be destroyed so that hypocrisy and exploitation would disappear with them.

Capetillo, like the anarcho-syndicalists, believed that the only powerful weapon against the exploitation of the workers was the labor movement. She insisted that "Organization is the only tool we have to defend ourselves against the present system. It is the only way to fight the injustices being committed against the workers, who produce everything."[8] She went further than the anarcho-syndicalists when she asserted that organizing was not only a means of obtaining short-term goals, but also was the most effective means to achieve a general strike which would reclaim all the workers' rights which had been abrogated by the "egotism" of the "tyrants." Once again she repeated the political doctrines of anarchism, which are anti-egotism, because anarchists considered egotism a negative expression in a so-called civilized society. In her book, *Mi opinión*, referring to the image of a peasant girl she sees tilling the soil in the countryside of Arecibo, she eulogized work with an almost religious fervor while accusing the landowners of being egotists, "Oh! Beautiful symbol of work and perseverance, I salute you in the name of universal brotherhood! And you, monstrous exploiter, measure your steps, because if you don't, you may fall into the precipice of your own egotism or into the abyss of your own errors!"[9]

Anarchism is also anti-fatalistic because it asserts that fatalism violates individual freedom. "Natural men and women" tend toward voluntary association based on the practice of mutual support. As she interpreted anarchism, she understood that workers would voluntarily join federations and cooperative organizations, solving the problems of the "new man" and the "new woman," without the need for authoritarian governments. The organization that Capetillo favored was the *Federación Libre de Trabajadores* because she viewed it as the vehicle through which the ultimate goals of the workers could be achieved. She urged them to organize with the rousing message, "This is why the workers must unite under the red flag of the *Federación Libre*, to defend their rights and to enjoy a better world, in greater harmony with reason and true justice. Workers, join the Federación Libre!"[10]

In her work *Ensayos libertarios*, Capetillo was virulently anticlerical, but profoundly religious. She expounded upon her ideas about "self-government" or independence for Puerto Rico from the United States. The essence of her opposition to independence came from her anarchist philosophy, since anarchism is, in its purest form, the idea of brotherhood and equality among all people. Therefore it is understood that anarchists should oppose all separatist movements, like nationalism or separation by race, religion or social class. She accused the "*Unionistas*," members of the Union Party of Puerto Rico—a group which in its first electoral program favored independence for the Island—of distrusting their own brothers in Puerto Rico, as well as in the United States. She also accused them of being "egotists, exploiters and

aristocrats," of supporting slavery for the workers and of being hypocrites who preached freedom, but freedom only for a few. They asked
for self-government, Capetillo said, for a Puerto Rico where the majority were the ignorant victims of the Union Party leaders themselves.
"Let us not be deceived," she said. "They ask for freedom and they
practice oppression." [11] She concluded by saying that Puerto Rico does
not need self-government, but rather adequate and substantial salaries
and compulsory education for all. In spite of the fact that Capetillo's
work is eminently internationalist in content, it is bound to an essential
Puerto Ricanness. Whether it be in personal allusions or references to
particular social problems, her love for Puerto Rico's needy children
and her devotion to its workers are ever present.

It is not a coincidence that Arecibo, at the beginning of the century,
was perhaps the most progressive city in Puerto Rico with respect to the
labor movement. Around 1904, under the red flag of the *Federación Libre
de Trabajadores de Puerto Rico*, Arecibo was the town with the highest
number of organized unions (twenty eight according to the FLT's direc-
tory), including a female union, the *Unión de Escogedoras de Café* (Coffee Pickers Union) Number 11600, and a union of female agricultural
workers with 3,000 members. The FLT's workers from Arecibo, according to Puerto Rican historian Angel Quintero Rivera, were also the first
to concern themselves with other aspects of workers' progress, beyond
issues of economic struggle.[12] In a union assembly the Federation from
Arecibo adopted the following resolutions: to establish an elementary
school at the FLT's headquarters; to create a body of volunteer teachers to offer primary instruction at the union locals for agricultural and
city workers; to address a petition to the City Council requesting a lot
to construct a building for the Federation; and to establish a price-con-
trolled city bakery.[13] It is not known if Luisa Capetillo collaborated in
the efforts of the Federation of Arecibo to establish schools for workers,
but the idea was consistent with her own desire to see education available to all.

In 1908 Capetillo participated in the Fifth Workers' Congress of the
Federación Libre de Trabajadores, where she defended female suffrage
with zeal, not only for women who knew how to read and write, but
for all women, without exception. In this Congress, she showed herself
to be a true suffragist, with more advanced ideas than those of the other
women, who later, in their own professional and civic groups, would
support the vote only for women who could read and write. Her fellow
workers in the labor movement on the Island considered her the "First
true suffragist in the country."[14]

At that time, however, neither Luisa Capetillo nor her sister workers in the labor struggle were focusing their efforts on the suffragist cause, since their main struggle was labor organizing.[15] In her detailed book, *El obrerismo en Puerto Rico* (The Labor Movement in Puerto Rico), doña Igualdad Iglesias de Pagán offers concrete data about the active and militant participation of women at the beginning of the labor movement in the early twentieth century. An important contingent of women joined the protests that the *Federación Libre* organized in Río Piedras in 1901 against the poor economic conditions of the workers. Of the fifty-seven people arrested by the police, eleven were women. In 1904, at the headquarters of the *Federación Libre* in Ponce, labor leader Ramón Romero Rosa delivered a lecture on *"La mujer obrera organizada"* (Organized Women Workers).

Capetillo was not alone in providing female leadership at the beginning of the century. Sister labor leaders included Concha Torres, the first Puerto Rican woman to speak at a workers' rally, and Paca Escabí de Peña, who wrote the article *"Nuestra Misión"* (Our Mission), in the pamphlet *Páginas del Obrero* (Workers' Pages), published by the Typographers' Union, Number 422 from Mayagüez, commemorating International Workers' Day in 1904. Paca Escabí was also one of the female leaders who served as a delegate to the Third Congress of the FLT, June 18-24, 1905 in Mayagüez. At that meeting a commission to organize women was formed. From then on, the Commission was included in all labor congresses. At the Third Congress resolutions were also approved to "declare the strike of the Ladies' Union in 1906" and to "request a legal workday of six hours a day for women." When the leaders of the Federation attended rallies or made speeches, they always addressed themselves to "male and female workers," and it was the custom to refer continually to the workers of "both sexes."

In 1909 Capetillo took part in the *Cruzada del Ideal* (Crusade for Workers' Ideals), a radical labor union tour under the sponsorship of the *Federación Libre*, which sent different groups of labor leaders to organize and advocate for support of their union. They went on horseback, by train, and on foot, visiting the countryside, holding workshops and talking with the workers. Capetillo visited Isabela, Aguadilla and Mayagüez, where she attended meetings of the Executive Council and the Joint Advisory Board of the Tobacco Unions. They also held a meeting on July 14th, Bastille Day, in celebration of the French Revolution, one of the most significant events in the emancipation struggle for women. When she returned to Arecibo she spent some time with her children and from there went to San Juan, where she met with several intellectuals and journalists, among them the well known writer and editor Mariano Abril. She published another edition of *Ensayos libertarios* to take to the factories. From San Juan she traveled to Caguas, where she met with the workers J.B. Delgado and José Ferrer y Ferrer as part of the *Cruzada del Ideal*. She spoke to the workers there and later in Juncos and Gurabo. When she returned to San Juan she was once again called to Arecibo to participate in union activities with the Utuado tobacco workers. In one of her stays in San Juan she became a distributing agent for the FLT's newspaper, *Unión Obrera*, and published her own magazine, *La Mujer* (Woman), which we have not been able to locate.

In 1910 she published her second book, *La humanidad en el futuro* (Humanity in the Future), published by the *Tipografía Real Hermanos* print shop in San Juan as an author's edition, under the editorial name of *Biblioteca Roja*. The book contained two essays, "*La humanidad en el futuro*," a lengthy work, and "*La educación moderna*," a shorter piece. The first essay—which takes up almost the whole book—was written on September 18, 1910, to make money to continue the publication of her magazine, *La Mujer*, and to establish a publishing house. In this essay Capetillo sketched her ideal for an egalitarian society in which priests, judges and lawyers would be unnecessary. Since the official church would no longer exist, the priesthood would disappear, supplanted by profound religious and Christian feelings. Similarly, judges and lawyers would no longer be needed, because there would be no crime and no legal contracts of any kind.

She believed that a general strike would serve as the foundation for a new vision of humanity. It would first be declared by ten workers, then little by little, thousands of workers and peasants would join them to form a new order based on a deeper sense of community. This community would be supported by mutual aid, and with the creation of consumer cooperatives it would be self sufficient in both material and intelectual ways. A Strike Committee would organize food warehouses, a bakery, collective kitchens, shoe stores, clothing warehouses, its own tailor shop, printing shop, and art and calligraphy workshops. Writers, artists, journalists, lawyers, scientists, doctors and all other professionals would learn to cultivate the land. Doctors would prescribe a "natural" lifestyle that would help prevent illness. Alcohol, tobacco, coffee and meat would gradually be eliminated from the community members' diet. Preventive medicine would be practiced instead of conventional medicine. "In this way," envisioned Capetillo, "all these communists would have their lives taken care of through their work for the community and would enjoy complete happiness."[16]

In ten years, this community that began with ten people, would multiply to more than 11,000, and its Strike Committee would turn into a Revolutionary Committee. The bourgeoisie—who would be bereft of services, workers to exploit, delinquents to accuse, and marriages to sanction—would request a meeting with the Revolutionary Committee. The Committee would state the rules under which the bourgeoisie, in an organized way, would hand over their material goods to the community and then be subjected to a process of education from which they would emerge cleansed of their previous social conditioning. Reverting to a state of "natural man" and "natural woman," they would join the communist society. Future society, according to Capetillo's conception, would have no use for government officials or politicians because there would no longer be egotism or power struggles. Everyone would perform his or her job in society in such an organized manner that it would not be necessary to have soldiers, policemen or jails. In her simple style, devoid of sophisticated literary devices, perhaps even pedestrian, Capetillo offers her analysis of contemporary society as she envisioned it, as well as the ideals she struggled for and dedicated her life to.

In *La humanidad en el futuro* she concisely explains her anarchist theory and her vision of the world. For her, anarchy is a lifestyle where each human being is responsible for his or her own existence, while at the same time concerned for the welfare of the collective, thus eliminating the need for rules imposed by a superior power. Each human being is considered a separate entity, entering into voluntary and individual association with thousands of other human beings, always respecting the rights of the others as if they were their own. For her, anarchy is the supreme organization of the universe.

It is difficult to talk about the theories of anarchists without talking about their personal lives, since their ideals are not merely a political system but rather a reflection of a lifestyle. It is apparent that the same idealism which determined Capetillo's political ideas also ruled her daily life. Because she demanded so much of herself, at times she suffered disillusionment and disappointment from expecting so much of others. In her ideal society human beings would always come together for love, without legal contracts. Luisa once again became involved in a relationship, this time with a pharmacist from Arecibo with whom she had a child. Already legally married, he never recognized the child. Luisa named him Luis, and he remained with her until the end of her life, adopting his mother's anarcho-syndicalist philosophy.[17]

It is clear that during the first decade of the 1900s Capetillo studied and learned extensively from anarchist thinkers from all over the world, as well as from her Puerto Rican anarchist *compañeros* who were in daily struggle to organize the workers. She internalized anarchist theories and interpreted them for Puerto Rican society, making them her own. Her analysis of society was directly based on Puerto Rican society, and the solutions were housed under the flag of the FLT of Puerto Rico. She was not interested in writing for the few, but rather for the greatest number of Puerto Rican workers. Her words did not merely live on the printed page, but represented the way she lived her entire life. She believed in labor organizing, since she herself was an organizer and an activist for the FLT; a vegetarian and devotee of naturalism, she advocated a return to nature in diet and lifestyle. She preached free love and had relationships with men without legal ties. Her beliefs in universal fraternity and the eradication of national barriers and borders inspired her to visit other countries, allowing her to share her ideals far beyond the limits of Puerto Rico.

NOTES

1. Capetillo, *Mi opinión*, 186.
2. I refer the reader to the writings of the Puerto Rican worker and union leader, *Memorias de Bernardo Vega*, ed. César Andreu Iglesias (San Juan: Ediciones Huracán, 1977), 59–60. In English, *Memoirs of Bernardo Vega. A Contribution to the History of the Puerto Rican Community in New York* (New York: Monthly Review Press, 1984). Also illuminating were conversations about the factory readers with Félix Ojeda, worker and former president of the Communist Party of Puerto Rico.
3. Gary R. Mormino and George E. Pozzetta, *The Immigrant World of Ybor City, Italians and Their Latin Neighbors in Tampa, 1885-1985*. (Florida: University Press of Florida, 1998), 103. These authors extensively interviewed many readers whose memories are very relevant to Luisa Capetillo's experience as a reader.
4. See Igualdad Iglesias de Pagán, *El obrerismo en Puerto Rico* (Palencia de Castilla: Ediciones Juan Ponce de León, 1973).
5. Capetillo's debut as a labor organizer appears on two contradictory dates, 1905 and 1907. I tend to believe it was in 1905, since various references situate Capetillo immersed in the workers' movement by 1907.
6. Capetillo, *Influencias*, 75.
7. Santiago Carreras, "¡Luisa Capetillo ha muerto! Por tu historia y por tu vida," *Unión Obrera*, Año 21, No. 87, April 15, 1922, 1.
8. Capetillo, *Ensayos libertarios*, 23.

9.   Capetillo, *Mi opinión*, 167.
10.   Capetillo, *Ensayos libertarios*, 32.
11.   Ibid., 33.
12.   Angel Quintero Rivera, ed., *Lucha obrera en Puerto Rico* (San Juan: CEREP, 1972), 72.
13.   Igualdad Iglesias de Pagán, op.cit., 295.
14.   Don Combas, "Prudencio Rivera Martínez," *El Mundo*, October 12, 1962, 2.
15.   In 1919 and 1920 the women of the Free Libertarian Federation of Workers actively participated in the suffrage movement, but never alongside the suffragists from civic or professional organizations.
16.   Capetillo, *La humanidad en el futuro*, 10.
17.   Luis Capetillo participated in the creation of the Partido Popular Democrático (PPD) in the early 1940s and was active in the labor struggle in Puerto Rico. He later moved to New York where he lived the rest of his life. In 1975, I went to his apartment in the Bronx in an attempt to speak with him. His wife informed me that he was not interested in being interviewed.

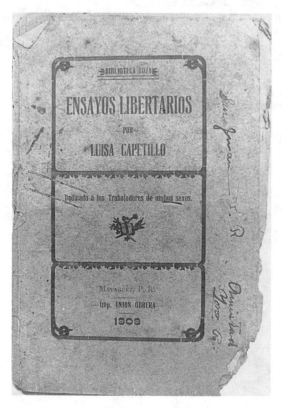

Fig. 5. Cover, Ensayos libertarios, 1909.

CHAPTER IV

The First Feminist Manifesto

1911 was an important year in the life of Luisa Capetillo. In addition to giving birth to her third child, Luis, she published her book of feminist theory, *Mi opinión*, about women's freedom, and their rights and duties as partners, mothers, and individuals. Published by her own editorial house, *Biblioteca Roja*, the book reveals her personal opinions about the condition of women, formed from her readings, but more importantly, from her own experiences. Her concerns centered on the premise that women are complete human beings with almost no freedom. She believed that the prevailing subordinate condition of women can and does persist because of women's ignorance and enslavement. But, as Capetillo was also a realist, she was honest with herself and her readers about the contradictions between her opinions and the realities of the society in which she lived. She never lost sight of the fact that her ideas were visionary and not always well received or understood in her historical milieu.

Her beliefs about the role of women at home, in the family, and in government coalesced in the first chapter of *Mi opinión*. Women should be educated, not only in the area of household chores and the art of making clothing, but also in science, arithmetic, geography and world literature. She asked herself incredulously, how was it possible that on the one hand, women were given the responsibility of bringing up children, and yet on the other, were denied access to liberal education. Capetillo believed that women should be educated so that they could teach their own children correctly, gain their husbands' and partners' respect, and in case of separation or divorce, be prepared to take over the financial and intellectual responsibilities of the home. These ideas, articulated in her own unique voice, clearly demonstrated the influence of the noted Puerto Rican educator Eugenio María de Hostos.

This feminist thinker repeatedly made it clear in her book that women and men should come together always for love, without any legal contract, and not for familial conventions, in a relationship encompassing respect and mutual support. There should never be a double standard where a man can be unfaithful to his wife, while she has to stay at home in a living situation where she is clearly inferior. Capetillo believed that marriage should be for love and be based on love. If one of the two falls in love with someone else, the union should be dissolved, but in a way that ensures the integrity of both parties. The woman should not be abandoned, but rather placed in a new role, educated to work in a satisfying job, and ready to join her life with another human being. This is one of Capetillo's most advanced ideas, that a woman could have the choice to voluntarily dissolve a union that doesn't satisfy her, whether it be to form a relationship with a man she loves more, or to maintain her own freedom. The idea that a woman could be properly prepared to work for a salary, in case of a voluntary or involuntary separation, is also a very progressive concept.

Capetillo believed that the education of girls and women should not be stereotyped. She felt that the educational curriculum should not limit certain subjects to girls, and others to boys. She favored exposing both sexes to a libertarian education in all subjects, the sciences, the arts, as well as physical education, gymnastics and calisthenics. Since she believed that marriage should not enslave women, she did not condone work that enslaved women. Her writings describe how deeply she was affected by the misery of female workers and how she exhorted them to organize. She believed that a communist society would allow for the creation of a new family structure, free from the traditional restrictions that suppress women.

Capetillo's belief in free love caused the greatest controversy in her time, was the most misunderstood and still confuses people today. To fully understand it, it has to be seen within the overall context of anarchist thinking. Free love was an obligatory concept for all anarchists of that era. According to anarchist doctrine, the most direct way to liberate human beings was to emancipate them from all legal contracts that limited their innate nature. To the anarchist, "free love" meant spontaneous love, or a relationship between two human beings, totally free of legal restraints. "Free love" was defined as responsible and voluntary love among competent and free adults, not sexual licentiousness. Emma Goldman, the well known Soviet-American anarchist and a contemporary of Capetillo, was also a faithful exponent of the theories of free love and sexual education. The anarchists considered sexual education a prerequisite for free love, because they undersood that only a person who has studied a subject and is informed about it can act freely.

In Puerto Rico, theoreticians Venancio Cruz, author of *Hacia el porvenir* (Towards the Future) and Angel María Dieppa, author of *El porvenir de la sociedad humana* (The Future of Human Society) discussed "free love" and placed it in opposition to marriage, which they deemed a legal contract that prostitutes women.[1] Consistent with the Romantic Movement, both authors idealized the prostitute and explained that poor women became prostitutes by necessity, to provide for their children or mothers, while marriage was the real prostitution, where young virgins were sold to men who could pay for their favors. Ideas about free love and contraception were popular at the end of the nineteenth century throughout Europe and within the progressive sectors of the American proletariat. In France, anarchist Emile Armand even affirmed that "marriage is long-term prostitution and prostitution is a short-term marriage." In the United States, Emma Goldman, who recommended that women "open their mouths and keeps their wombs closed," was arrested for publishing and promoting free love and contraception.[2]

Luisa Capetillo's chief influence on the subject came from journalist, poet and French educator Madeleine Vernet. Vernet, whose essay, "Free Love," Capetillo included in her book, *Mi opinión*, was the editor of the anarchist magazine *La mère educatrice* (Motherhood and Education). She established teaching centers in France, like those of Francisco Ferrer in Barcelona and Sebastian Faure in Paris, which were models of modern education. [3] For Vernet, marriage, love and desire were three different issues. Marriage was a social convenience, an imprisoning entity, a prostitution of love. Love was passion, the union of emotion with intellect, while desire was a mere carnal need. Both Vernet and Capetillo worked to educate women about their sexuality so that they could distinguish what is desire and what is love, and thus satisfy both needs responsibly. They understood that the dominant belief of their day was that only men had sexual and emotional needs, and consequently women were condemned to live unsatisfying and infertile lives. Their aim was to empower women so that a woman's sexuality would not be subordinate to men's, and women could be free to express their feelings.

Her ideas about love and sexuality have been proven over time to be profound and visionary. Preaching what was considered sexual heresy engendered much antagonism and great personal anguish to Capetillo. Even some of her more enlightened comrades were suspicious of her ideas on sexuality although they supported them on a theoretical level.

On occasions they made sexual propositions to her, arguing that if she preached free love, she should practice it by having sexual relations with them. In a notebook that she used as a diary in New York around 1919, Capetillo commented that a comrade whom she considered her friend, continuously harassed her, demanding sexual favors. She wrote, "I saw Manuel Hernández from Arecibo, who as usual started with his nonsense and impertinences, but finally gave up. I made him stop and he left by himself. I went home alone; it was about eleven."[4] In a letter, she answered an anarchist friend from Panama, who, although he claimed to be her friend, confessed his sexual attraction each time he saw her in person. Capetillo explains to him that she understands his desires but cannot reciprocate, since she has other goals to achieve and doesn't want to "disturb my spiritual peace, in other words, I would rather channel my sexual energy to strengthen my mental prowess."[5]

Other anarchist comrades, however, did support Capetillo's feminist ideas, at least theoretically. Julio Aybar, editor of the newspaper *Unión Obrera*, said that her theories did not intimidate him. "We are not threatened by anything that Capetillo says in her book because they have always been our own opinions. Luisa breaks with today's hypocrisy and faces the issues with courage, fearless about what she writes, since it seems to us that she practices what she preaches."[6] With the publication of *Mi opinión*, Luisa Capetillo became the first Puerto Rican woman to organize her feminist ideas and publish them as a theoretical document. Even though there are admitted contradictions in the book, she felt compelled to analyze the status of women in its totality, influenced by their physical, intellectual and emotional condition, as well as social environment.

Where do Capetillo's ideas fall within the context of feminism in Puerto Rico? As an advocate of equal education for women, education without limits, Capetillo demonstrated her solidarity with the early struggle that impelled women and men to support the advancement of women. Nevertheless, by the first decade of the twentieth century, it is my opinion that feminist ideas in Puerto Rico were divided into two ideological currents. The first was reformist, which was promoted mainly by professional women and men from the upper classes who almost exclusively worked for the intellectual development and empowerment of women through education and later, for women's suffrage. The other, the workers' current, advocated economic and human rights via the emerging labor movement. This group comprised female and male workers in the needlework industry, the tobacco industry, and agriculture, all of whom fought to organize the female workers into unions. In their union, the women fought for better salaries, shorter working hours, and a series of protective laws for both women and children.

Luisa Capetillo belonged in the second group. Although she supported and promoted education for women, she believed that attaining workers' rights through awakening the consciousness of both female and male workers, would have a more immediate effect on larger numbers of people. In spite of the fact that the working class also supported women's suffrage, and demanded it for all women, even if they were illiterate, her priority in life was union organizing. In principle, Capetillo supported women's suffrage, and defended it in a Congress of the FLT, but it was not a priority in her daily struggle or in her philosophy of life. In her writings there are no allusions to the topic, or evidence that she joined any feminist groups organized on the Island, aside from those in the labor movement.

In 1917, while Isabel Andreu de Aguilar, Mercedes Solá and Ana Roqué, among others, were organizing the *Liga Femínea Puertorriqueña* (The Puerto Rican Women's League) to fight for the vote, Luisa Capetillo was leading the agricultural workers' strike in Patillas and writing for the newspapers. Despite the fact that she did not belong to any autonomous feminist group, her writings offered advanced thinking on the subject. Her position in favor of universal, non-discriminatory education, equality at work, and women's control over her own body through the knowledge of her physiology, made her a progressive woman for her time. She worked in a male bastion—the labor movement—while a single mother; she was educated and independent, intellectually and economically; she was motivated by a deep feeling for social justice; and was passionate about exercise, vegetarianism, and esoteric subjects such as reincarnation and spiritism. Capetillo could easily be a protagonist in the re-emergent feminist struggle of the 1970s, although she lived at least a hundred years earlier.

While Luisa Capetillo theorized about women and anarchism in Puerto Rico, her contemporaries did the same in many other countries, among them Argentina, Mexico, Uruguay, Spain and the United States. Juana Belén Gutiérrez (1875-1942) in México, María Collazo (n.d.) in Uruguay, Juana Rouco Buela (1889-1969) in Argentina, Voltairine de Cleyre (1866-1914) in the United States, and Teresa Clamunt (1862-1931) in Spain, preached the emancipation of women and free love and fought for workers' rights while living lives consonant with their ideals. They all used journalism and public speaking to promulgate their ideas, each one from her own perspective. Although they were in solidarity with the international workers' movement, it is not known if they knew about each other. What we do know is that they were all visionaries and feminist pioneers in their countries.[7]

In 1912 Capetillo moved to New York, as Puerto Ricans did at that time, living there for a short period. She became involved with the Hispanic community, particularly with the cigar workers, who actively embraced and promoted her anarchist ideas. She collaborated with the anarchist newspaper *Cultura obrera* (Working Class Culture), *Brazo y cerebro* (Muscle and Mind), and *Fuerza consciente* (Conscious Power), publishing articles about female emancipation. "*La mujer*," one of the articles that she published in 1912 in *Cultura obrera*, was later included in the anthology, *Voces de liberación* (Voices of Liberation), published in 1921 by Lux Editorial from Argentina. Printed for the purpose of gathering the libertarian voices of the most progressive women in the world, the book contains short essays by Rosa Luxembourg, Clara Zetkin, Emma Goldman, Louise Michel, and various Latin American women including Margarita Ortega, a Mexican revolutionary, María López from Buenos Aires, and Rosalina Gutiérrez from Montevideo. The editorial note introducing the authors states, "These voices of liberation are a call to women by their own *compañeras* to think more and act together with men in the struggle for human emancipation."[8]

In 1913, in solidarity with the workers' movement, Capetillo moved to Ybor City, Florida, where there was an important Hispanic colony, mainly of tobacco workers. Ybor City was founded in 1885 as a tobacco factory town, home to hundreds and later thousands of tobacco workers—cigarmakers and tobacco leaf strippers—and their families. They came mainly from Spain and from Cuba, which was experiencing its Ten Year Independence War against Spain. The young city was named for Vicente M. Ybor, founder of a tobacco empire in Cuba. His descendent, Vicente Martínez Ybor, was one of the two founders of Ybor City. The other founder was a Spaniard named Ignacio Haya, whose factory was originally located in New York City, and then moved to Ybor City. The Cuban and Spanish workers, as well as an amalgam of men and women from other Caribbean countries, mainly Puerto Rico and the Dominican Republic, were an alert and politically conscious work force. They soon developed their own unions, schools, cooperative banks, publications and study groups as well as social clubs. Anarchism and socialism were the cornerstones of their life, while their revolutionary ideas were their daily bread. They demanded to be informed daily about what was happening in Cuba. The institution of the reader was as important in Ybor City as it was in the other cities and countries that housed tobacco workers and their unions. José Rivera Muñiz in his book *The Ybor City Story, 1885-1954* comments that "The cigar factories became without doubt the most efficient places for the dissemination of the ideal of independence. The readers in the cigar factories...carried out a task worthy of praise".[9] He acknowledges the work of the readers, singling out several well known Cuban readers by name. Luisa Capetillo lived and worked in Ybor City. It is unknown whether she worked as a reader while living there, but she probably did, since she was recognized for her work as a reader in Puerto Rico.[10]

In Ybor City Capetillo wrote much of the material that would later become her book, *Influencias de las ideas modernas* (1916), while also producing a more polished second edition of *Mi opinión*. She saw herself and her movement as extending beyond national identity. "Freedom is my country. Truth is my motto. Universal fraternity is my goal."[11] In the prologue to the second edition of *Mi opinión*, Jaime Vidal, an anarchist living in the United States, praised Capetillo for her written and practical work in support of the proletariat of the world, especially women. He supported Capetillo's theory of free love, confirming its place in anarchist philosophy. About Capetillo he wrote, "For me, the author of this book is one of the most independent and free women of the Hispanic-American race, and when discussing free love she is imbued with the fiery and poetic expression of Latin writers and the ease of Anglo-Saxon thinkers. She enriches her theories and criticism with an abundance of arguments that convince even the most skeptical in the matter of free love."[12]

Cuba was the next stop in Capetillo's itinerary. She lived in Havana and in Cárdenas, where she once again interacted with the tobacco workers and the leaders of the strong and vital anarchist movement on the sister island. In 1915 a sugar cane strike broke out in Cuba and spread over many of the island's provinces. The *Federación Anarquista de Cuba* (Anarchist Federation of Cuba), representing twenty-four groups, circulated a manifesto that aggressively censured the government's attitude and showed solidarity with the workers on strike.[13] The document, signed in Cruces, was known as the *Cruces Manifesto*. As a result of her solidarity with the Manifesto, President Menocal considered her a dangerous foreigner and ordered her deportation.[14] There is no record of whether the deportation order was actually carried out, but in July of that same year, the Puerto Rican anarchist made news and entered the public opinion arena when she was detained for a bold, unrelated action: dressing in a man's suit.[15]

On July 24, 1915, Luisa Capetillo walked down the street in Havana wearing pants, a shirt, tie, jacket, and a short brimmed hat. On Neptuno Street, M. Rodríguez, a guard from the Third Precinct Police Station, detained her for "Causing a Scandal" and took her to the Second District Corrections Court, presided over by Attorney García Solá. The guard testified before the judge that he detained Capetillo because he thought her eccentric way of dressing was attracting passersby and causing a scandal. In court, where a large number of people had gathered, the Puerto Rican anarchist defended herself, stating that it was her understanding that pants were more hygienic and comfortable, and were also more appropriate for women in their new role. She said she had walked through the streets of Puerto Rico, Mexico, and the United States in pants, and had never been bothered before.[16]

According to the extensive coverage of this event in Caribbean newspapers, Luisa Capetillo asserted in her own defense, "Your Honor, I always wear pants," and lifting her dress slightly, showed a pair of loose white pants that almost reached her ankles. She continued, "And on the night in question, instead of wearing them underneath, I wore them just like men do, based on my perfect civil right to do so, on the OUTSIDE."[17] The Havana newspaper *La Lucha*, in contrast to other papers in the city, treated the incident seriously, without sarcasm. The brief editorial entitled "A Brave Female," praised her daring, though it did describe Capetillo as a woman "who loved doing things inappropriate for her sex."[18] The newspaper reported that she was acquitted. The press used the Capetillo incident to ridicule the anarchists, accusing them of always trying to draw attention to themselves. One of the Havana newspapers, *El Día*, published an enormous photograph of Capetillo dressed in pants. The same photograph was also published in Puerto Rico.

The pants incident should not be interpreted as a superficial event in Capetillo's life. As we have previously emphasized, she, like every true believer in the anarchist philosophy, acknowledged the intimate connection between intellectually advocating anarchist ideals and embodying them in daily life. For Capetillo, wearing pants and men's suits represented her defiance of traditional institutions, moral standards and bourgeois ethics. Her arrest was calculated and typical of many anarchist actions designed to shock conventional society, to take advantage of the impact of publicity, and create forums to further advance her goals. Her actions were not unprecedented. Once in Paris, during the summer of 1905, an anarchist speaker showed up dressed only in a bathing suit. He was arrested for indecent exposure, but was acquitted when he testified and showed it was scientifically proven that sweating while dressed in heavy clothing retains bodily toxins, causing discomfort and even disease in human beings. The speaker accomplished his dual purpose: to defy social conventions of the era and to have an impact on society through publicity.[19]

The French case, just like the Capetillo incident in 1915, occurred during the golden age of anarchism in Europe and America, between 1880 and the second decade of the twentieth century. Enabled by the invention of the airplane, automobiles, and enhanced communication media, such as the movies and inexpensive newspapers, the era possessed a unique immediacy and dynamism never before seen, directly reflected in the strikes and actions of the proletariat and their progressive causes. In their time, the anarchists were also dynamic, original and creative. Historian Roderick Kedward explains, "Their performances shocked police in every country, their spectacular actions filled the newspaper headlines, and their mystique of struggle and revolution surpassed other progressive doctrines.[20]

Although Luisa Capetillo was never arrested in Puerto Rico, she scandalized its citizens by using not only split skirts but also harem pants and tapered pants that were only worn by men at that time. A journalist from the San Juan newspaper *El Imparcial* commented that Capetillo was not discreet in wearing pants. She was determined to wear them and to explain their virtues to anyone who was hostile to her or tried to ridicule her. "She never vacillated. She put on men's pants and just took to the streets. It was a monumental scandal."[21] Almost fifty years after her death, labor leaders and contemporaries still remember her as the first woman in Puerto Rico to wear pants in public. Historian Angel Quintero Rivera comments, "When we asked the old labor leaders about her, all of them—without exception—began by mentioning that she was the first woman in Puerto Rico to wear pants or pantskirts…"[22] Doña Carmen Rivera de Alvarado in her article, "Women's Contribution to the Development of Puerto Rican Nationality," recalled that when Capetillo visited a town, people would attend the meetings held by the Socialist Workers Party, which Capetillo belonged to, not so much to hear her speeches, but to see the first woman to wear pants in public. According to Rivera de Alvarado, "Even though she wore pants, she gave the impression of being a woman from head to toe, and no one—that I'm aware of—ever doubted her femininity."[23]

Capetillo was progressive in her outlook and practices regarding dress, health and diet. She wrote, "Pants adapt perfectly to this era of female progress."[24] She also recognized the value of using light and airy fabrics for dressing in the tropics. In her own diet Capetillo was a vegetarian who believed meat contained toxins harmful to the body. She favored a diet mainly of fresh fruits and vegetables, cheese, whole wheat bread and milk. In 1919, when she lived in New York, she rented various rooms in her apartment on 22nd Street and Eighth Avenue to fellow workers, to whom she also served vegetarian meals. At the frequent social gatherings held there, they not only talked about anarchism and the proletarian struggle, but they also ate very well, according to the memoirs of *ilustrado* (enlightened*) cigar maker Bernardo Vega, a frequent participant.[25] In addition to having a boarding house and a restaurant, Capetillo was a reader in a cigar factory in New York and also actively participated in the public debates addressing the question of class struggle. She was so committed to the workers that she fed everyone who came to her house, even if they had no money to pay. Not surprisingly, her business suffered the same financial difficulties of similar proletarian businesses.

In 1918, in the aftermath of the infamous earthquake which shook Puerto Rico, the New York newspaper *La Prensa* took up a collection to aid the thousands of poverty-stricken victims. Faced with the readers' meagre response, the newspaper published an editorial complaining about the lack of concern on the part of the community for poor Puerto Ricans, many of them workers on strike at that time. The crisis generated a great deal of discussion. Capetillo insisted that the government was responsible for the poverty that existed in Puerto Rico, and that it was important for progressive North American workers to be made aware of the situation. She concluded, reflecting the classic anarchist position on nationality and the motherland, "Tyranny, like liberty, has no country; neither do exploiters nor workers." Vega remembers that during these years Luisa Capetillo seemed noticeably tired. Perhaps the tuberculosis that would ultimately undermine her health was already present in this woman who lived life so intensely.

In 1916 Capetillo published her fourth book, *Influencias de las ideas modernas*, containing several plays, as well as short stories, letters, memoirs and poems. In this work she demonstrated a maturity in her advocacy for the emancipation of women and also refined her writing style. She dedicated a good portion to recommendations that would enhance her readers' lives. These included vegetarianism and meditation, inspired in the Far East. She condoned drinking and smoking only

---

*Translator's Note. "Enlightened," in this instance, refers to the workers who were educated through participation in group study, study by themselves, reading theoretical and political books, militancy in the union, and being read to in the factories.

in moderation, and advised young people that instead of seeking a life of luxury, ribbons and lace, they should exercise and follow a regime of personal hygiene. "To be progressive and call yourself civilized, it is necessary to do a little exercise and bathe daily..."[26] Her ideas on nutrition, exercise and meditation did not distract her from her active role in the labor movement; on the contrary, she rose to a leadership position in the agricultural workers' strike in Patillas in 1917, where she was clubbed by the police during the demonstration.

In 1918 Capetillo and Domingo Santos Cruz from Ceiba, directed the activities of the agricultural workers' strike in the eastern part of the Island that included the towns of Ceiba, Naguabo, Fajardo and Luquillo. The strike attracted more than 30,000 workers who were members of the *Federación Libre de Trabajadores de Puerto Rico*. Her work, as described in letters to FLT leader Santiago Iglesias Pantín, was to direct the activities of the strikers in their rallies, and in their organizational, educational, and cultural meetings, as well as in labor and political meetings held in preparation for the strike. She organized protests, massive demonstrations and rallies along the coast. There is no record as to who negotiated the workers' demands with the bosses, or what changes resulted from the strike, however, it is known that this agricultural workers' strike worried the U.S.-appointed Governor of Puerto Rico, who talked with Iglesias Pantín about the situation. Capetillo and Santos speculated on the possibility of bringing a demonstration of more than 30,000 rural workers to the gates of La Fortaleza, the Governor's official residence and office.

On March 29, 1918, at the height of the strike, Capetillo, who directed the marches on horseback, dressed in pants, was arrested and jailed together with three other workers on the charge of inciting a riot. Capetillo tells Iglesias in her daily letter to him that early that afternoon a policeman screamed at her, "'You're going to jail and you've got it coming to you!' I was on horseback, wearing pants, and I would stop to talk to the *campesinos* who were coming and going, and they stopped the car that the policemen were riding in..."[27] Capetillo was detained that night. The police shoved her and harassed her until they reached the station where she was jailed. In the police blotter, the guard José Huertas wrote:

> Around 8:50 P.M. today, in front of *La Federación Libre* on Main Street of this town, the socialist agitator, Luisa Capetillo, white, a native of Arecibo, and about 34 years old, and Santos Cruz, a 52-year-old mulatto, native of Ceiba, incited and advised a large number of people in said *Federación* to commit violent acts and to disobey and attack the police, these acts being related to

the present agricultural workers' strike in this municipality.[28] (See the complete text in Appendix C.).

Bail for Capetillo was set at $400, a large amount for that time. She was freed when bail was paid by some of her fellow workers from that area. After the strike ended, the trial was set for June 10. Domingo Santos sent a telegram to Capetillo, who at that time was living on Magallanes Street in Arecibo, urging her to be at the trial since the *compañeros* who posted bail for her were all poor. Capetillo then wrote to Alonso Torres, Secretary of the FLT, asking him to send her money so she could attend her trial in Ceiba. There is no information about the outcome of the trial since efforts to obtain a transcript from the Office of Judicial Administration of Puerto Rico were unsuccessful.[29]

1919 was a very active year for Capetillo. She took part in the agricultural workers' strike in Vieques, where she was attacked by strikebreakers. A journalist stated in *Unión Obrera*, "…she showed her temper of steel at the Vieques strike where she was attacked by mobs paid by the capitalists. Her serenity was unshakeable…"[30] During that time she also visited the capital of the Dominican Republic, Santo Domingo, where the shoemakers were on strike, demanding a salary increase. Capetillo was invited by that country's *Federación Libre de Trabajadores* to be a speaker in an event organized by the strikers. The censor demanded that her speech be submitted in advance. Because Capetillo refused to be censored, she was forbidden to speak in public in Santo Domingo. She did, however, help the workers collect money so that their families could survive. José Casado R., Secretary of the *Federación Libre de Trabajadores de Santo Domingo*, dedicated May 1, 1922, International Workers' Day, to the memory of "the most virile fighting woman who shared the hardships of the struggle for our well-being with us and identified with the suffering of the miserably enslaved people."[31]

Apparently during this time Capetillo commuted between New York and Puerto Rico, participating in union activities in both places. At that time, a major area of concern for her was the creation of an Agricultural Farm School for Puerto Rico's poor children. She tried to enlist economic support from Samuel Gompers, president of the American Federation of Labor, and moral support from various distinguished Puerto Rican figures. Santiago Iglesias Pantín, however, refused to support the project because he felt that the money should come from the Puerto Rican people, not from the United States.[32]

Like the majority of the anarchists of her time, Capetillo was deeply impressed by the victory of the revolutionary forces in Russia in 1917.

From that moment on she nurtured the hope of visiting the USSR.[33] In the 1930's, the western world witnessed the decline of the anarchist movement. Progressive European forces were overwhelmingly supportive of the new Soviet Workers Republic. Many anarchists requested admission to the USSR, and Ogarev and Herzen saw their work published there. Emma Goldman and Alexander Berkman returned to their native homeland, Russia, only to repudiate it a few years later for what they considered to be the "dictatorship" of that implacable state. In Puerto Rico too, anarchist ideas and their influence on the labor movement declined. Some were attracted by the Soviet Union, others by the militant labor movement in the United States, directed by the charismatic Gompers. The FLT of Puerto Rico became affiliated with the U.S. organization, and from that time on, the Puerto Rican labor movement would be tied to the American labor movement, which would effectively halt the anarchist and socialist ideas that gave it life in its early stages.

In 1920 Capetillo participated in the election campaign of the Socialist Workers Party, even though doing so meant an apparent contradiction of her anarchist ideals. The classic anarchist position was to take power through a spontaneous revolution, as Bakunin believed, or through a general strike, as Capetillo believed, and not through a vote. She participated in rallies in support of the candidacy of Santiago Iglesias Pantín, whom she admired and considered her comrade. Along with the group of workers who participated in the campaign was the young Luis Muñoz Marín, who later became prominent in the political life of Puerto Rico. History does not offer any testimony or opinions from Capetillo herself about her brief participation in the political elections, since by that year her writings did not appear as frequently in the workers' newspapers.

While living in a small house in Buen Consejo, still under construction in the recently created workers' neighborhood in Río Piedras, she suddenly suffered a serious tuberculosis attack. On April 10, 1922, accompanied by her youngest son, Capetillo entered the Municipal Hospital in Río Piedras, where she died a few hours later. A delegation of her companions from the *Federación Libre* in Río Piedras accompanied her body to her humble house. A day later she was buried in the municipal cemetery of Río Piedras. The funeral orations were delivered by her companions Alfonso Torres, Florencio Cabello, Esteban Ortiz and José López. Her children, Manuela, Gregorio and Luis, only a child at the time, were also present. With deep emotion, Santiago Carreras describes the moment, "Her funeral was a poor one, as is always the case with apostolic leaders of the great causes of humanity."[34]

Luisa Capetillo lived intensely and actively from the moment she became part of the labor struggle to the moment of her hospitalization and death. She fought for proletarian causes, education for the masses, and the emancipation of women. Her life was not easy or pleasant. She had no comforts or luxuries. She inspired hostility in many people who rejected her revolutionary ideas. However, it is also true that until her last moments, she was accompanied and comforted by the workers, her *compañeras* and *compañeros*, to whom she offered her life. In her confessional book, *Influencias*, she bemoans the envy and rancor that those who fight for truth and justice suffer. Yet this Puerto Rican anarchist clearly never regretted her life's direction, aptly describing herself as "a stoic of life…"

NOTES

1.   See note #30, Chapter I. Among other Puerto Rican anarchist thinkers who wrote about free love are José Ferrer y Ferrer and Rafael Alonso Torres, labor leaders who were ideological and activist comrades of Capetillo.

2.   See Kedward, 106-107. I refer the interested reader to the autobiography of Emma Goldman, *Living My Life* (New York: Dover Publishers, 1930) and the Richard Drinnon biography, *Rebel in Paradise, A Biography of Emma Goldman* (New York: Harper Calophon Books, 1961).

3.   Francisco Ferrer founded *La Escuela Moderna* (The Modern School) in Spain, and Sebastian Faure founded *La Colmena* (The Beehive) in France. Modern Schools were also founded in the United States, in Chicago and in New York. A source for further information on these progressive projects is *The Anarchist Encyclopedia*, found on the Internet.

4.   Capetillo, unpublished notebook, unpaginated.

5.   Capetillo, *Influencias*, 67.

6.   "Luisa Capetillo," *Unión Obrera*, 16 de noviembre de 1911.

7.   For further information on these anarchist feminists see Voltairine de Cleyre, *The Voltairine de Cleyre Reader*, ed. A.J. Brigati, (California: AK Press, 2004); Norma Valle-Ferrer, "Anarquismo y feminismo: la ideología de cuatro mujeres latinoamericanas de principios del Siglo XX," *Revista Cultura*, Instituto de Cultura Puertorriqueña, San Juan de Puerto Rico, junio de 2004; for Teresa Claramunt access: http://www.alasbarricadas.org/ateneo/mudules/wiki-mod/index.php?page Clamunt (retrieved July 30, 2005) and http://www.tvcatalunya.com/històriesdecatalunya/personatges/per107681437htm (retrieved July 30, 2005).

8.   *Voces de Liberación* (Buenos Aires: Editorial Lux, 1921), unpaginated.

9.   Jose Rivera Muñiz, *The Ybor City Story, 1885–1954* (Tampa, Florida, 1976) 36.

The author asserts that all readers were Cuban, but does not identify his sources. In addition, the book was published by the translators Eustacio Fernández and Henry Beltrán in 1976, but the date of the original text is not offered in this edition, although we can infer it was 1954 based on various comments by the author.

10. I visited Ybor City in 2001. It has become a museum honoring the history of the tobacco industry, although devoid of its revolutionary fervor. The visitor can still see some of the machinery used at the tobacco factories and there is a wonderful small wooden building that houses a facsimile of a tobacco stripping factory with the elevated platform for the reader. I envision Luisa Capetillo there, reading animatedly to the workers.

11. Capetillo, *Mi opinión*, second edition, unpaginated.

12. Jaime Vidal, "Dos palabras" in *Mi opinión*, 1.

13. "Violenta protesta anarquista," *Heraldo de Cuba*, January 22, 1915, 2.

14. León Primelles, *Crónica cubana, 1915–1918* (La Habana, Cuba: Editorial Lex, 1955) 78-79.

15. Ibid., 113.

16. In reference to this incident, I found evidence in Capetillo's own words that she had visited Mexico, however, I have not been able to corroborate this fact.

17. "El caso de la mujer con traje masculino en la Corte Correccional," *Heraldo de Cuba*, July 27, 1915, 1.

18. "Una brava hembra…," *La Lucha*, July 26, 1915, 1.

19. Kedward, op. cit., 103.

20. Ibid, 5.

21. "La muerte de Luisa Capetillo," *El Imparcial*, April 12, 1922.

22. Quintero Rivera, op. cit., 34.

23. Carmen Rivera de Alvarado, "La contribución de la mujer al desarrollo de la nacionalidad puertorriqueña," in *La mujer en la lucha hoy*, eds. Nancy Zayas and Juan Angel Silén (San Juan: Kikiriki, 1972).

24. Capetillo, *Mi opinión*, 150.

25. Vega, *Memorias*, 149.

26. Capetillo, *Influencias*, 96.

27. Luisa Capetillo in a letter to Santiago Iglesias Pantín, Ceiba, March 30, 1918.

28. Puerto Rican Police Records, Ceiba, 1917-1918, 144.

29. To obtain a transcript of the trial I contacted the Office of Judicial Administration of Puerto Rico and was told that the records had been destroyed in a fire.

30. "Luisa Capetillo," *Unión Obrera*, April 13, 1922.

31. "20 de Mayo," *Justicia*, May 29, 1922.

32. Ibid.

33. Unpublished letters from the Archives of the FLT: Luisa Capetillo to Santiago Iglesias, May 16, 1919; Iglesias to Capetillo, May 30, 1919.

34. Manuel Ríos Ocaña, "La muerte de Luisa Capetillo," *La Correspondencia*, April 12, 1922.

35. Carmelo Rosario Natal, *La juventud de Luis Muñoz Marín* (Hato Rey: Master Typesetting de Puerto Rico, 1976), 116.

36. Carreras, op. cit.

Fig. 6. Luis Capetillo, youngest child of Luisa Capetillo, who took her surname, on Condado Beach in Santurce.

CHAPTER V

Capetillo's Impact
on the Social Conscience of Puerto Rico

The era in which Luisa Capetillo lived represents the turning point in the historical development of women in Puerto Rico. In her written works and in her militant activity as a labor organizer, she espoused the most advanced principles of the nineteenth century and the most radical principles of the twentieth century. Her intellectual and social development did not occur in a historic void, but rather was a result of enlightened ideas about women's status that were being developed since the second half of the nineteenth century. As we have seen, the central issue of education for women allowed liberals to transcend class barriers and join with the workers who also sought to open the perennially closed doors to education.

Capetillo, however, lived the life of a woman on the edge, marginalized by a society imbued with conservative ideas and limited by archaic traditions that assigned women an inferior role, subordinate to masculine authority. Although in Puerto Rico there was discussion of the liberal ideas of Alejandro Tapia y Rivera, and later, of Eugenio María de Hostos, it was Luisa Capetillo who established a new precedent by living according to her revolutionary ideals. By daring to live her own way, she was severely punished by the society she was forced to exist in. Among her peers, her lifestyle was resented by even the most progressive workers. Nevertheless, Capetillo was inspired by and steeped in her parents' readings and their adherence to the Romantic Movement. Embracing the anarchist principles that excited many Romantic European minds, she was able to live a different life with great bravery.

Her ideal was to achieve a communist society where all human beings would be equal, with every worker equally valued and none being more privileged than others. She envisioned a community devoid of exploiters profiting from the labor of the workers, the major producers in society. Her books, *Ensayos libertarios* and *La humanidad en el futuro*, clearly articulate these thoughts, as well as outline her religious concerns. Luisa Capetillo fought against the dominant social system. As part of the nascent labor movement in Puerto Rico, she rebelled against the misery, exploitation, and inferior conditions women endured. As an agitator and political activist, she traveled throughout the country and abroad, spreading the message to fight for workers' rights. Her internationalist solidarity took her to Cuba, the Dominican Republic and the United States. Despite what is known about her activities, it is difficult to measure Capetillo's importance in the development of the Puerto Rican labor movement because the known historical sources are scarce. Additionally, because of the deeply ingrained prejudice existing against women, we cannot measure, with any accurate historical perspective, the true extent of her participation in the strikes of Patillas, Ceiba and Vieques, for example.

There is no doubt that Luisa Capetillo was the first woman to successfully challenge prevailing prejudices against women by becoming an important labor leader and advocate for women and the poor. The workers of Puerto Rico recognized that she was indeed a woman ahead of her time. They respected her spirited words and her unique lifestyle, even though they did not always share her ideas. Her home was always a magnet for progressive discussions in New York as well as on the Island.

Elderly workers I interviewed, who knew her, remembered her for her indomitable bravery. There was no scarcity, however, of comments ridiculing her way of dressing (which was considered brazenly masculine), or other remarks that expressed resentment towards her radical stand on sexual education and free love, as well as criticism of her contradictions. In her own life, and even after her death, she evoked the rancor of conservatives who believed that "poor Luisa was plowing the sea," a description by a journalist in an article in *El Mundo*, who stated that no woman would follow the revolutionary principles of the *boricua* anarchist.

Decades after her death, nevertheless, judgment can be passed on her theories about women, contradictory though they may be in some instances, but clear and defined at other times. In the evolution of ideas, few concrete goals are ever achieved immediately, but over time it has been proven that Luisa Capetillo's influence on the progressive development of Puerto Rican women was profound and extensive, and continues to resonate to this day.

By-laws of the Ladies Association for the Education of Women, 1886

Letter from the Presidency

Designated by the article of the By-laws of the Ladies Association to preside over the Board* of which I am honored to be in charge, and hoping that the highly patriotic and beneficent intention to instruct and educate women will be well received and extend itself as much as possible throughout this Province, during my directorship, I have not hesitated to address myself to you as the highest Authority of this town, to implore you, along with the town priest, to call upon all those people who are known to have feelings of Christian charity, without distinguishing political differences, with the purpose of, and according to a reading of the By-laws that I include, installing the Board, duly elected from among the attending men and women to whom Article 6 of the By-laws refers.

Given who you are, I have good reason to expect that my request will be attended to as soon as possible; the President who is elected should send me a note indicating those who were elected by the Board, outlining their respective duties.

May God keep you many years.

Puerto Rico, February, 1886

Countess Verdú

Government of the Island of Puerto Rico
Office of the Secretary
Fifth Bureau No. 829

To the Very Esteemed Governor General by decree of this date, and in compliance with the information of the Provincial Board of Public Education; the Regulations by which the Ladies Association for the Education of Women will govern itself have been hereby approved. In accordance with the orders of Your Excellency, I include for your information a copy of the aforementioned proposal.

May God keep you many years.

Puerto Rico, December 4, 1885

Angel Vasconi
President of the Teachers Association

Foundation of Professor
don José Cordovéz y Berríos
Lares, Puerto Rico, 1885

Principles

Article 1. Mindful of the remarkable expansion in women's education and instruction in Europe and America, a far reaching movement is being encouraged by individual and societal initiatives, by municipal and provincial associations and by national governments. This Society, under the protection of ladies and young girls of the upper classes, is being established in Puerto Rico with two objectives: one, modest, given the present economic situation that the Province is experiencing, and the other, more ambitious, focusing on the future.

Art. 2 The actual objective of this Association is to provide "to daughters of poor and middle class families who have a vocation for teaching," the means to obtain a professional education and instruction, and the degree that is required by the law to direct a Public or Private school.

Art. 3   In the future, when the resources allow it, this Society will extend its aegis to finance the following special areas of education: Business, Telegraphy, Typography, Bookbinding, Obstetrics, and others suitable to the intelligence and education of women.

Art. 4   To fulfill the first objective of this Association, it will place the candidates in the respective vocational departments of the Model School.

Art. 5   When any of the Model Schools does not meet the necessary pedagogical conditions concerning the teaching resources and supplies, the candidates will be placed in the Girls Schools established by the Societies promoting education.

Art. 6   A local Board in each town will be in charge of the government of this association. The Board comprises women, with the exception of a male bookkeeper and an assistant secretary. The Boards of the District Heads will have the character of Departments; and the Board of the Capital will act as the Board of Directors, whose current President is the honorable Countess Verdú.

Each local Board will be composed of:
   A President
   Two Vice-Presidents
   A Treasurer
            Two Consultants or Board Members
            Two Auxiliary Consultants
            A Bookkeeper
            A Secretary
            An Auxiliary Secretary

It will be divided into two sections under the direction of the two Vice-Presidents: one, a Division of Finance, in charge of everything having to do with collecting money, bookkeeping, remittance of funds; and the other, a Division of Taxes, in charge of requesting subsidies, memberships, collection and the remittance of objects for the Bazaar and Exhibitions of the students' work, and the delivery of books donated to the Municipal Library. The Bookkeeper and the Auxiliary Secretary will be paid for their work.

Art. 7   The resources of the Association will consist of:
1.   Membership dues.
2.   Subsidies granted by the City Halls, Provincial Delegations, Central Government, The Royal Economic Society of the Friends of the Nation, and the Ateneo.

3. Grants that other corporations or philanthropists want to make, whether it be in money, or in objects that can be used in a bazaar or raffle, or books for the Municipal Library, or flyers, pamphlets, and written works by the donors themselves on the advantages of women's education to the progress and well-being of the country.

4. Money earned from the theatrical productions to support the Association.

5. Money earned from contests, conferences, and evenings that are held in honor of the Association.

6. Money resulting from the Bazaar that will take place, according to special regulations, with donated objects.

7. Money from the exhibits of the students' work that will take place annually, also under special regulations.

8. Inheritances and legacies.

9. Refunds that the educated girls are able to return to the Association for the cost of their education, when by virtue of their professional preparation, they obtain jobs; such refunds will be modestly fixed by the corresponding local Board.

10. Interest earned on the funds collected trimestrally by the local Board or Board of Directors.

Art. 8   Each trimester the local Board will send to each of the District Boards and then these Boards will send to the Board of Directors—with the proper security and under joint responsibility—the funds collected and the verified accounts of office expenses, collected funds, and other funds consigned in the budget; the documentation of which and the money sent would be corroborated in the corresponding receipts.

Art. 9   The Board of Directors will place those quantities above mentioned under its responsibility in the general Treasury of student savings, once the general Treasury is established. Meanwhile the Mercantile Credit Corporation of the capital, or another bank, will trimestrally publish the amount of the taxes being paid, in the newspaper *Public Education*, with an indication of how much each Department and each local school receives. It will also annually publish the general account of income and expenses and a statement of the works realized.

Art. 10   This Association will be composed of the following kinds of members:

1. FOUNDERS – Women and men who in each town are elected to constitute the first local Board, also contributing with dues, elaborated in sections 6 and 7 of this Article. Also the regular

members and subscribers who contribute the quantity of ten dollars, one time.

2. EX-OFFICIO – The representatives named to oversee the investments of their respective corporations and intitutions. Cited in section 2 of Article 7. Also the Vice-President and Secretary of the Ladies' Board of the San Ildefonso Asylum, the Director of the Provincial Institute of Secondary Teaching, the Director of the Professional School, the Inspectors of primary teaching, the President of the Commission of Teachers Exams, the Secretary of the Provincial Board of Public Education, the Director and Secretary of the Economic Society of Friends of the Nation, the Presidents of the Board of Directors and the Department Boards of the Teachers Association, the Director of the Ateneo, the Director of the Societies promoting education, and the Directors of the Societies that foster the education of destitute children.

3. MERIT – Women and men who offer the Association a notable service for its importance and transcendence, which will be resolved legally, whose record will be referred to the Board of Directors for their decision. The notable services worthy of such valuable regard include the following and other analogous ones: 1- To cede to the Association a profitable piece of land, or a house in good condition, or the profits from such farms; or a quantity fixed with all the necessary guarantees or the interest from such a quantity; 2- To endow some girls' school with furniture and learning material, as long as this gift is considered important because of its value and pedagogical worth; 3- To pay for the books and clothing of some poor girls during their academic education on the school site; 4- To take the orphan girls and provide them with education and instruction either at home or in a school setting; 5- To pay for the professional career of one of the young girls who meets the requirements elaborated in article 2; 6- To pay the following expenses of one or more of the girls whom the Association protects: the trip to school, transportation to the exam, professional title and the return trip; or clothing, books, material, and other personal objects that the establishment requires for the personal life and education of the student; 7- To submit for the benefit of this Society any unpublished work about the advantages of teaching women, or any didactic work with respect to any of the subjects taught to women; 8- To have been a teacher, with good evaluations, for twenty five years; 9- To distinguish themselves by

the number and importance of the books donated to the local city Library, including their own works, for the education of women; 10- To give the Association, and through them, to the Library of the Royal Economic Society of Friends of the Nation, the collection of works published by Puerto Rican authors in or outside Puerto Rico, including those from collections of old and new newspapers, published in Puerto Rico. In addition, the people who, in or out of the provinces, distinguish themselves for their service to Instruction, Welfare, or Hygiene, and the City Halls that excel in granting subsidies, which are referred to at the end of the Paragraph 2, Section 4 of this Article.

4. PROTECTORS – 1- The Government, the Provincial Delega-tion, the City Halls, the Royal Economic Society of Friends of the Nation, the Ateneo, and the Societies or Circles of Welfare, Instruction or Recreation, by means of their annual subsidies; 2- Individuals, who in their local neighborhoods, in agreement with the parents, seek the establishment and maintenance of private schools for girls through written agreements that would consist of the number of girls to be admitted, the fee that would be paid for each one, which will be gradual if more than one girl from the same family and domicile attends the school; the person who will provide, free of charge, the site for the classes and a room for the teacher, or those persons who will contrib-ute to its construction in the most central place and in the best hygienic conditions, and in this case, the person who will be in charge of sustaining the teacher's expenses until she becomes self supporting through the success of the school, etc., etc. The category of Special Members will include those individuals who distinguish themselves in the fostering of rural schools, and also those teachers who admit poor girls from the neigh-borhood to their schools, or the City Hall that subsidizes these endeavors; 3- Individuals, who from time to time contribute to the development of the town Library, donating books, maps, charts, or any other learning material; 4- Individuals, who of-fer prizes for literary works about the education of women, or who pay for the prizes that are mentioned in the By-laws or the Programs of the exhibits of students' projects; 5- Individu-als, who by their constancy, distinguish themselves in donating objects for the Bazaar and those who distinguish themselves by requesting and collecting such gifts; 6- Individuals, who pro-mote and conduct contests, soirees, and lectures for the benefit

of this Association; 7- Individuals, who seek with devotion and efficiency to vaccinate as many people as possible and to fulfill the laws of hygiene in their place of residence; 8- Journalists, who in their publications spread the advantages of the instruction and education of women and reproduce, for publicity purposes, the minutes and accounts of this Association; 9- Teachers, who send their students' work to the exhibits, thus earning the title of Special Members; and those who distinguish themselves for their constancy in donating gifts to the Bazaar.

5. HONORARY MEMBERS – The founders of Societies that foster the education of destitute children, and Societies that promote education for women; also individuals from Spain who send books to be distributed to the town Libraries and the women and men who, as parents, find themselves within the exception referred to in Sections 6 and 7 of this Article.

6. REGULAR MEMBERS – If at least one lady from a family or residence offers her patriotic assistance to this society, she will pay a twenty-five cents membership fee; just seven and a half cents for the membership fee for two ladies; if there are three ladies, they will pay twelve and a half cents for two memberships, and fifteen cents for three memberships, if four or more join. A mother who has more than three regular members in the society, from her family or residence, will be exempt from paying the membership fee. She will be exempt from paying the monthly fee. In this case she will have the title of Honorary Member.

7. SUBSCRIBERS – Gentlemen who contribute to their membership fee with fifty cents and a gradual but doubled monthly fee as fixed to the regular members. A father who has more than three regular members from his family or residence will be exempt from paying the membership fee. In this case he will have the title of Honorary Member.

Art. 11 The ladies and gentlemen that belong to this Society can use the emblem that the Board of Directors will establish.

Art. 12 This Association will subsidize Aid Societies that foster the education of destitute children in consideration of the noble intentions of these agencies. These institutions will distribute among themselves the five percent of the annual fees from the subscriber members. The five percent from the fees of the regular members will go to the San Ildefonso Girls School.

Art. 13 One year after the establishment of the local Board, the Board of Directors will calculate the number of young ladies they can support at these establishments, after taking into consideration the available and financial reports from the Model Schools and the Girls Schools. In a solemn public session, prior to the beginning of the courses, they will designate, by means of a public drawing, the towns that should send a candidate.

Art. 14 The towns that will be eligible to enter the public drawing will be those on the first two thirds of the list, in numerical order from the most to the least funds collected up to that date, including more than one town tying with the same low amount of funds and those towns whose funds differ from the last ones by one to ninety-nine cents.

Art. 15 Once the public drawing has been verified and the results are published, the local Boards of the chosen towns will propose the young lady worthy of the protection of this Society. If there is more than one they should propose the most outstanding candidate, based on her intelligence and effort. They should ask for a report from the local Board of Education. If both young ladies are equally prepared, one should be chosen by a lottery in a public session.

Art. 16 When one or more positions become vacant because of the absence of candidates, or by death, or the interruption of the career of one of the students, the Board of Directors will hold a special drawing to fill the vacancies. The towns already chosen and those that said they didn't have a candidate at that moment will be excluded. The drawing will include those towns on the list whose funds were so low that they could not enter the regular drawing.

Art. 17 When the funds allow an increase in positions, or they have to fill certain vacancies because a student has completed her education, the Board of Directors shall proceed according to Article 14 to designate positions by means of a regular drawing. Later, according to Article 16, any special drawings that are necessary will be held.

Art. 18 At the Department of Public Education the ruling legislation states that in order to obtain the title of teacher, the girls should be at least twenty years old, and have taken between one and three courses in teaching. The candidate should not be younger than 17 years old. Meanwhile, the Board of Directors requests and receives from the government, the enforcement of Article 53, Paragraph 1, August 27, 1882 of the By-laws of the Central High School for Teachers that states, "In order to register in the elementary course, the student must be at least 15 years of age and no more than 30."

Art. 19 Once the local Boards are divided into the two sections mentioned in Article 6, each section will be divided into special committees depending on the number of issues to be resolved.

Art. 20 Once the local Boards are established and organized, each one will draw up their own by-laws and submit them to the Board of Directors for their approval, which will be granted, if they do not affect what has already been established.

Additional Article – Concerning the Presidency, the By-laws state that the President shall be the Governor General's wife who, if unavailable or absent, will be temporarily and annually substituted by the Vice-Presidents, according to age. In addition, when Her Excellency, the Countess of Verdú vacates the Presidency, she will become Honorary President.

Lares, May 26, 1885, - Saturnina Arana de Arana, - Rosa Arana de Cordovéz. - Prudencia Roig de Arana. - Carolina Arana de Cordovéz. - Amelia Arana y Arana. - Isabel Serrano de Méndez. - Herminia Storer de Vilella. - Joaquina Vélez de Vilella. - Orosia Serrano de Pol. - Ruperta Pol y Serrano. - Amelia Pol y Serrano. - Julia Torres y Pol. - Rosa Torres y Pol. - Margarita Torres y Pol. - Teresa Coll de González. - Adelina Acevedo de Méndez. - Eulalia Vega de Luigi. - María de Jesús González y Pérez. - Elena González y Pérez. - Rita Medina de Ferrer. - Rita María Ferrer y Medina. - Laura Ferrer y Medina. - Felipe Arana, landowner. – Gregorio María Cordovéz, farmer. – Virgilio Arana, farmer. – José Carlos Arana, farmer. – Aurelio Méndez Martínez, landowner and merchant, City Hall Representative. – Pablo Vilella, landowner, merchant and Second Deputy Mayor. -Jose Vilella, landowner, merchant and elected City Councilman. - José María Torres, landowner. – José González y Hernández, landowner. – Juan Lingi y Domenech, merchant and City Councilman. – Manuel F. González, landowner and elected City Councilman. – Tomás González Rodrígiuez, professor. – Aurelio Méndez Serrano, professor. – Virgilio Acevedo Hernández, merchant and elected City Councilman. – Bernabé Pol, landowner. – Justo Méndez Martínez, landowner, merchant and City Councilman. – Jorge María Ferrer y Medina. – José Monroy, landowner, City Councilman. – Antonio Collazo, landowner, merchant and elected City Councilman. – José Cordovéz y Berríos, professor and City Councilman.

---

* Translator's note. We have maintained the liberal use of capital letters found in the original nineteenth century texts.

Fig. 7. Don Manuel Ledesma, Marquis of Arecibo, was the great love of Luisa Capetillo's life and the father of her children, Manuela and Gregorio.

Selections from
Influencias de las ideas modernas, 1916

Why say...

Why call George Sand a wild woman in the publicity for her books? I protest the use of such an inaccurate epithet for such a cultivated and intelligent woman. It is not worthy of educated people. Why do we have to call women who are on a higher moral plane than men, prostitutes and corrupt?

I see queens, empresses, intelligent women whose reputations demand redress because their behavior and conduct has been exaggerated in an abusive way. Why accuse a free woman like Anne Boleyn of being a prostitute, and others, whom I won't mention, since their relatives are still alive?

The only reason for historians to exaggerate the behavior of women from other eras was because of the preponderance of men, and the fact that they were the legislators, historians and keepers of all sciences, arts and literature. They are used to flattering themselves with exaggeration, to exalt and elevate reputations while they ignore cultivated, free and educated women, believing that these women are inferior and not capable of realizing original intellectual work.

I refuse to accept the assertion of any historian who erroneously believes that women have no right to use their freedom without being considered corrupt or immoral, while men have been able to do whatever they want and indulge the most absurd and ridiculous whims, without being judged, repudiated or prevented from going where they choose, with no concern about not being paid attention to, respected or sought after. We are going to put an end to those unequal laws—where the few have a lot and the many have a little—in order to finally secure peace for the just and achieve the truth and justice that our sex deserves.

March 22, 1914

Visions

Suddenly, I heard a sound, like an immense clamor of an agitated crowd, very far away...

There wasn't really a disturbance where I was standing that could justify that perception, but I heard it clearly and distinctly in my ears. At that moment the memory of the French Revolution came to my mind, as if I could see the convulsive crowds passing by in an impressive roar, crossing Rivoli Street on their way to the Bastille... Ah! How wonderful that moment was but how painful for me when I remembered in successive visions the weeping of that poor boy, mistreated by Simon... Poor Simon, how much will that weigh on his conscience now! What kind of fault was it of that poor, weak creature?... When even his parents were innocent. His only fault was the profound error of tradition!

Oh, people! Masses that stir, demanding justice that they have yet to know! Demand it! Demand your rights, enforce them if you will! But respect the weak, the innocent who are guilty only of having received an inadequate education! Eliminate power but not people. You have no right to suppress lives that you did not create. Violence can never be mother to freedom, only its stepmother. Education is the mother of freedom; science is her eldest daughter; and her sisters, tolerance and discretion, with rights and responsibilities.

New York, August 26, 1912

———————

I saw a huge lion, wearing a crown stained with blood and blackened by fire, streaking through the green and beautiful countryside, the clear air illuminated by the sun's rays. In spite of its weight, the crown kept sliding off the beast's beautiful head, and in front of a steep cliff, the orb tumbled into the inscrutable abyss, precipitated by a movement that made the lion stumble.

The lion, surprised when he realized that he no longer bore the weighty circle, shook his mane and breathed heavily, making the mountains and the prairie tremble with his roar. Climbing on a rock, he sat there, majestic and conceited, challenging the star-king with his mane, and licking his round and gleaming haunches. The lion had broken with the tradition that made him wear the crown and…

I saw an eagle, that taking flight proudly crossed the sky, displaying the imperial crown. A cloud emerged, shaped by a swirl of bullets from a city. It confuses the eagle, who surrounded by it, falls wounded by a shot. As she falls, the crown tumbles, is hit, breaks and is soiled; and the dying eagle is taken to a palace. The eagle's wounds heal, but she will leave without the crown. It is the imperial eagle of Germany.

I saw another beautiful eagle standing on a rock, contemplating the lovely panorama of Moscow. The eagle descends, is taken prisoner and led to a cell by armed henchmen. An immense cloud hides the city. The bullets cross and the eagle dies. It is the Russian imperial eagle. Another popular symbol emerges and the land is divided or distributed.

———————

I never used carriages, wore jewels, lived in palaces, wore silks or ornaments, nor dazzled misery with the insulting luxury of jewelry and superfluous things. I scorned honors and rejected privileges. I ignored adulation, nor would I allow begging. All of this, in the middle of great abundance, and without having studied the social question, I believed that everybody had the right to be clean and clothed, to wear shoes, and I didn't understand why it wasn't so. I thought everybody knew how to read and write and I was astonished when I saw the opposite. Ignorance, mistress and lady of the world, holding souls prisoner and consciences in darkness. Inscrutable abyss whose door was the Church, that has left its mark on the generations of twenty centuries! Because I was no slave, I protested against that denigrating legacy, by not taking my children to the contaminated baptismal font.

———————

I…

(To the artist Manuel García, San Juan)

I am mistaken. I believe I have the right to enjoy everything created by Nature, everything invented by man in the arts, industry, mechanics, astronomy, etc. and to observe everything that has been discovered by scientists.

But I only use what is necessary and I almost always reject the superfluous. Generous to a fault, indifferent to vanity, luxury and riches. Sometimes, to remind people that I have the soul of an artist, like almost every woman does, I dress up, but without ostentation. And if I weren't such an anarchist, that is, "so Christian," I would dress splendidly, artistically and with exquisite taste. But what about the less fortunate who lack the necessities? The hungry, the naked?... How cruel! What sarcasm! Although we are all brothers, some die of hunger and others foolishly waste their excess, and every day invent a new luxury, while what is useful and necessary rots at the depots and warehouses of foodstuffs, clothing and shoes. And with so many naked and barefoot!...

I... helpless to relieve such misery! Oh! My great worry is the problem of poverty. Meanwhile, this mad woman advocates equal rights for everybody, brotherhood and the abolition of laws and governments. Difficult things! Instead of prisons, I would have schools, art and vocational academies, free trade, free love, the abolition of marriage and the substitution of private property for public property. An endless round of nonsense overwhelms us! Demands from the new era that is approaching. In spite of all this honesty, I have not been understood. On the contrary, I have been defamed and misinterpreted.

Men's opinion about women, and my own

Women should always be women! Women's work is her home! She should not be *macho*! Mend socks and shorts! Doze under the comforting lamplight knitting socks! Who asked for their opinion? Who asked them to get involved in politics or dare to run for office? That cannot be allowed! Haven't we already let them enter the sacred halls to become lawyers and doctors? Well, they're not satisfied. Now they want to become judges, mayors, chiefs of police or legislators. Is that why we let them study, so that they can push us aside, dare to take over our jobs and surpass us? I don't know how these women can forget how weak and indiscreet they are by nature. You can't trust them or teach them anything, because immediately, they want to take over. But how can woman imitate man? She can't, because she's inferior. Even Mother Nature condemns her to seclusion during childbirth and breast-feeding.

That's how men talk and that's their conception of women, forgetting all about their wives, mothers and daughters. But you don't have to be afraid that everything will be lost, or that these arguments will disturb the peace of the home, because a woman doesn't stop being a woman just because she's involved in politics or expresses her opinion, or becomes a legislator or a detective. A woman will always be a woman, whether she's a good or bad mother, whether she has a husband or lover. She's a woman, not only when she's powdered and wearing lace and ribbons, just like a man doesn't stop being a man when he learns to cook, mend, sweep and sew. How many men do that! Women do not pretend to be superior to men; at least that's not their intention. They will, however, surpass men by their acts and the fulfillment of their duties.

The immense majority of women do not smoke or get drunk. And this is one of the qualities that will make them superior in all human endeavors. So it isn't women's intention to imitate men, especially not their faults, but maybe their strengths and virtues. The other day I read that a young woman applied for the job of a steamboat stoker, and later the boss said, "She did a better job, and besides, she doesn't drink whiskey."

All this will benefit the human race. Women are preferred as nurses since men are really no good at it. Women will be preferred as doctors because of their values and the way they are. They will heal for love in order not to see suffering. Women will be preferred as lawyers because of their insight and persuasive skills. They will be preferred as legislators because their laws will correct the abuses against the unhappy workers and the wretched poor. Women will be preferred in politics because they will not sell themselves and they will keep their word. All of this, in general terms, and with few exceptions. Women will not invade the gambling dens, nor will drunkenness cause them to mistreat their husbands and children. Women don't want to invade men's terrain, where they would acquire their vices and abuses. A woman will always be a mother even if she doesn't have children. She will try to correct everything that might harm future generations.

Fig. 8. Manuelita Ledesma Capetillo, daughter of Luisa, in the senior citizens home she resided in. Carolina, Puerto Rico, 1974.

A Letter and a Police Report

Letter to Santiago Iglesias Pantín*

Ceiba, March 30, 1918

Comrade and friend Iglesias:

I just received your telegram at 8:30 p.m. Domingo is in Fajardo. Here are the reports. In my previous letter I told you about the meeting and about the enthusiasm of the *campesinos*. The next day, that is, yesterday, Friday, there were rumors that the police were going to kill a few strikers, that they were going to end the strike, etc... As long as nothing happens, I'm not worried. After dinner the Federation was filled with people, as was the street. I went out with Domingo and sent two telegrams, one for you and the other for Wanton. When we came back Domingo opened the meeting. I stayed outside watching, since there had been rumors that they were going to break in... Well, I walked around the Federation and on the opposite corner, next to the window in the dark alley, I saw some new men, among them a dark fellow I had seen on the road from Naguabo to Río Blanco, who said to me, "It's about time that you were thrown in jail." I was on horseback, in pants, and I stopped to talk to the *campesinos*, who were coming and going, and they stopped the car that all the policemen were in, because they didn't want to leave me behind, and when I turned around, they also backed up the car to hear what I was saying. So, I went back and told Juan Centeno what I had seen, and he said to me, "They've searched some of them and taken away their clubs." I said, "Who has the right to search here? What law gives them permission? Just like a house can't be searched without a warrant, they can't search the *campesinos* and take away their clubs."

I addressed the *campesinos* who were outside and I spoke in a very loud voice and told them, "How can you let them take away your sticks or clubs without protesting? That's really citizen abuse and you're all cowards." This was said in a loud voice, and the dark man said to me, "It's really about time that you went to jail." I tried to answer and he screamed, "Shut up!" and I answered, "Why should I shut up?" and he said, "You shut up!" and he pushed me violently and ordered them to arrest me while he pushed me. Officer Rodríguez already held me tightly by my arm, shaking me, and kept pushing me through the street until we got to the police station, and even after I was on the balcony he kept on pushing me. All the time I kept telling him, "Don't push me like that!" but it was useless, he just continued.

At the police station I kept on talking from the balcony so that they would tell Domingo, who didn't move from the meeting, as he told me later, so that people wouldn't leave. But someone named Cecilio Morales made a phone call to Soto from Fajardo and told him that bail was $400, and that Soto said, no matter how much it was, they had to bail me out. At 10:00 p.m. I got out and tried to make a phone call, but it was already too late. I headed towards the Federation, and although there was hardly anyone there, Santos had not moved. So, I tried to get those who were there to sing *The International* and to cheer up the people who seemed to be glued to the wall and to the benches. They told me that women, and men too, had left, running. To get them to move I had to personally go to each one myself, and say, "Come on, cheer up." And when I enthusiastically explained their rights as citizens to them, I heard someone in the street say, "Shut that woman up!"

Right then a policeman comes over and orders us to close up and leave. I answer him, "Why? Who gave the orders to close?" They had already closed the doors. One of the bondsmen comes up and says to me, "Oh, please, I beg you to obey, I put up your bail, and..." "Well, we better just look for another bondsman! But why are we going to close?" Then all the police answered at the same time, "Tomorrow you'll get to talk. We're going to close now." And those *campesinos*, so used to obeying without answering back, closed up, because they saw that the police were aiming their guns at them. Do you think they would have shot or opened fire? Of course not! It was to intimidate and frighten them and make them close up. But they'll pay for it, I assure you that I won't close this place and nothing is going to happen. But as you can see, this is the way these people are.

Listen, I forgot to tell you, that the excessively servile policeman F. Rodríguez searched me, and a while after my arrest the poor *campesinos* arrived and told me that the police had hit them. Now, tell me what I should do and how I should denounce these outrages, or if you're going to do it. This afternoon the boys from Fajardo came over and took me to Naguabo. We talked and came back here again. Tomorrow, Sunday, we'll have an all night vigil, so that Monday morning we can have a demonstration. We'll see what happens; we'll let you know.

(signed)
Luisa Capetillo

*Transcription of a handwritten letter from the Archives of the *Free Libertarian Federation of Puerto Rican Workers*.

Police Report*

Carmelo Correa
Log Book of the Police Department of Puerto Rico
Ceiba, 1917-1918, Pages 143, 144 and 145
March 29, 1918

Officer José Rodríguez #458, at 6:00 p.m., Officer José Huertas #327, at the police station, reporting that the following persons were arrested and jailed at 8:50 p.m. for having disobeyed the orders of the Police Chief in command, after a big riot provoked by the socialist woman (*La Capetillo*): Daniel Pacheco y Pacheco, native of Yauco, 25 years old, dark skinned; Enrique Ávila, native of Ceiba, 23 years old, white; Lino Gómez, native of Ceiba, 54 years old, black.

Elaborating upon the previous report, I add the following: around 8:50 p.m. today in front of the Free Libertarian Federation on Main Street of this town, the socialist agitator Luisa Capetillo, white native of Arecibo and about 34 years old and Santos Cruz, a 52-year-old mulatto, native of Ceiba, incited and advised a large number of people in said Federation to commit violent acts and to attack the police, these acts being related to the present agricultural workers' strike in this town. About 400 to 500 people with a menacing and aggressive attitude started to riot. We dispersed them without violence, arresting the following individuals who refused to leave the premises when the riot started: Daniel Pacheco y Pachecho, Enrique Ávila, Lino Gómez and Manuel Danois.

The Chief of Police of Fajardo was advised of the situation, and to prevent anything serious from happening he personally came here, and with the forces under his command ordered the dispersal of the militant groups and the closing of the Federation. Luisa Capetillo, who was released on parole, later returned to said Federation with the intention of provoking new protests and causing new breaches of the peace.

(signed)
Carmelo Correa
Corporal, Island Police

*Document in the National Archives, San Juan, Puerto Rico.

Chronology of Luisa Capetillo's Life

1879 October 28. Luisa is born in Arecibo, Puerto Rico.

1890 June 24. She is baptized in San Felipe Apóstol Cathedral in Arecibo.

1897 Her daughter Manuela is born.

1899 Her son Gregorio is born.

1904 She writes for newspapers in Arecibo.

1905 She makes her debut as a labor organizer. She starts working in the sewing industry.

1906 She works as a reader in the tobacco factories of Arecibo.

1907 She publishes her first book, *Ensayos libertarios*.

1908 She defends women's suffrage and the organization of women into labor unions.

1909 She participates in *La Cruzada del Ideal* (Crusade for Workers' Ideals) of the *Federación Libre de Trabajadores de Puerto Rico*.

1910 She writes and publishes her book, *La humanidad en el futuro*. She edits the magazine *La Mujer*.

1911 Her third child Luis is born. She publishes her book *Mi opinión*.

1912 She lives in New York City. She publishes articles and becomes active in labor organizations there.

1913   She lives in Ybor City, Tampa, Florida. She publishes the second edition of *Mi opinión* there.

1914   The Cuban government issues an order for her arrest and deportation, claiming she is a dangerous anarchist.

1915   She is arrested in Cuba for wearing pants in public.

1916   She publishes her book *Influencias de las ideas modernas.*

1917   She participates in the agricultural workers' strike in Patillas as a labor leader.

1918   She is arrested for disturbing the peace and inciting a riot during the agricultural workers' strike that she leads in Ceiba.

1919   She participates in the agricultural workers' strike in Vieques as a labor leader.

1920   She lives in New York, runs a boarding house and a vegetarian restaurant and participates in public life in the city.

1921   She participates in the electoral campaign of the Socialist Workers Party of Puerto Rico and also helps in the organization of the strike of Río Piedras workers.

1922   April 10. She dies of tuberculosis in Río Piedras, Puerto Rico, and thousands of workers attend her funeral in the public cemetery of Río Piedras.

Bibliography

Books

Alonso Torres, Rafael, *Cuarenta años de lucha proletaria*. Federación Libre de los Trabajadores. Imprenta Unión Obrera, Mayagüez, Puerto Rico,1905.

Angelis, María Luisa de, *Mujeres puertorriqueñas que se han distinguido en el cultivo de las ciencias, las letras y las artes desde el Siglo XVII hasta nuestros días*. Puerto Rico: Tipografía El Boletín Mercantil, 1908.

Avrich, Paul and Barry Pateman. *The Modern School Movement. Anarchism and Education in the United States*. California: AK Press, 2005.

Brau, Salvador, *Ensayos (Disquisiciones Sociológicas)*. Río Piedras, Puerto Rico: Editorial Edil, Inc., 1972.

Canales, Nemesio, *Glosario, antología nueva de Nemesio Canales, Tomo I*. San Juan, Puerto Rico: Editorial Universitaria, 1974.

———. *Meditaciones acres, antología nueva de Nemesio Canales, Tomo II*. San Juan, Puerto Rico: Editorial Universitaria, 1974.

Capetillo, Luisa, *Ensayos libertarios*. San Juan: Tipografía Real Hermanos, 1910. (Biblioteca Roja).

———. *La humanidad en el futuro*. San Juan, Puerto Rico: Tipografía Real Hermanos, 1910. (Biblioteca Roja).

———. *Influencia de las ideas modernas*. San Juan, Puerto Rico: Tipografía Flores, 1916.

———. *Mi opinión, sobre las libertades, derechos y deberes de la mujer como compañera, madre y ser independiente*. San Juan, Puerto Rico: Biblioteca Roja, 1911.

———. *Mi opinión, disertación sobre las libertades de la mujer*. 2da. Ed. Corregida. Ybor City, Tampa, Florida, Imprenta de J. Mascuñá, 1913.

Carr, E.H., *Los exilados románticos*. Barcelona, España: Editorial Anagrama, 1969.

Centro de Investigaciones de Sociales. Centro Coordinador de Estudios, Recursos y Servicios de la Mujer. *Participación de la mujer en la historia de Puerto Rico (Las primeras décadas del siglo 20)*. Rutgers, The State University of New Jersey y Consorcio para la Equidad en la Educación del Centro de Investigaciones de Sociales de la Universidad de Puerto Rico, 1986.

Chomsky, Noam and Barry Pateman, editors. *Chomsky on Anarchism*. California: AK Press, 2005.

Coll y Toste, Cayetano, *Historia de la Instrucción en Puerto Rico hasta el año 1898*. San Juan, Puerto Rico: Boletín Mercantil, 1910.

Comisión de Derechos Civiles, *La igualdad de derechos y oportunidades de la mujer puertorriqueña*. San Juan, Puerto Rico, 9 de septiembre de 1972.

Corretjer, Juan Antonio, *Para que los pueblos canten*. Guaynabo, Puerto Rico, 1976.

Cruz, Venancio, *Hacia el porvenir*. San Juan, Puerto Rico: Tipografía La República Española, s.f.

Cuesta Mendoza, Antonio, *Historia de la educación en el Puerto Rico colonial*. 2da. Ed. México. Imprenta Manuel León Sánchez, S.C.L. 1946-48.

Dávila Santiago, Rubén, *Teatro obrero en Puerto Rico (1900-1920) Antología*. Río Piedras, Puerto Rico: Editorial Edil, 1985.

De Cleyre, Voltairine, *The Voltairine de Cleyre Reader*. Edited by A.J. Brigati. California: AK Press, 2004.

De Quesada, A.M., Ybor City, *Images of America*. Charleston, South Carolina: Arcadia Publishing, 1999.

Díaz Soler, Luis Manuel, *Historia de la esclavitud negra en Puerto Rico*. Río Piedras, Puerto Rico: Editorial Universitaria, 1967.

Dieppa, Ángel María, *El porvenir de la sociedad humana*, Puerta de Tierra: Tipografía "El Eco," 1915.

Dolgoff, Sam, ed., *Bakunin on Anarchy*. New York: Vintage Books, 1972.

Drinnon, Richard, *Rebel in Paradise, A Biography of Emma Goldman*. New York: Harper Calophon Books, 1961.

Elzaburu Vizcarrondo, Manuel, *Prosas, poemas y conferencias*. San Juan, Puerto Rico: Instituto de Cultura Puertorriqueña(ICP), 1971.

Federación Libre de los Trabajadores de Puerto Rico, Su programa, leyes y cooperativas. San Juan, Puerto Rico: Press of the San Juan News, 1903.

FLT Unión de Tabaqueros, Actuaciones de la segunda y tercera asambleas regulares de las uniones de tabaqueros de Puerto Rico (Puerto Rico Publishing Company, San Juan, Puerto Rico) Balance General, 1907-1912. Tip. El Progreso, Bayamón, Puerto Rico, 1912.

Federación Libre de los Trabajadores de Puerto Rico, Tercer Congreso. Mayagüez, Puerto Rico: Imprenta Unión Obrera, 1906.

Ferrer y Ferrer, José, *Los ideales del Siglo XX*. San Juan, Puerto Rico: Tipografía La Correspondencia de Puerto Rico, 1932.

Ferrer Hernández, Gabriel, *La mujer en Puerto Rico*. Puerto Rico: Imprenta de El Agente, 1881.

———. *La instrucción pública en Puerto Rico*, 1885.

García, Gervasio L. y A. G. Quintero Rivera, *Desafío y solidaridad, breve historia del movimiento obrero puertorriqueño*. Río Piedras, Puerto Rico: Ediciones Huracán, 1982.

Godio, Julio, editor, *La destrucción del estado, Antología del pensamiento anarquista*. Buenos Aires, Argentina: Centro Editor de América Latina, 1972.

———. *Los orígenes del movimiento obrero*. Buenos Aires, Argentina: Centro Editor de América Latina, 1971.

Gómez Tejera, Carmen y David Cruz López, *La escuela puertorriqueña*. Sharon, Conn.: Troutman Press, 1970.

González, Nilda, *Bibliografía de teatro puertorriqueño (Siglos XIX y XX)*. Río Piedras, Puerto Rico: Editorial Universitaria 1979.

Griffin, Frederick C., editor, *Woman as Revolutionary*. New York: A Mentor Book, 1973.

Guerin, Daniel, Estados Unidos 1880-1950, *Movimiento obrero y campesino*. Buenos Aires, Argentina: Centro Editor de América Latina, 1972.

———. *El anarquismo*. Buenos Aires, Argentina: Editorial Proyección, 1968.

Hostos, Adolfo de, *Tesauro de datos históricos, Tomo II*. San Juan, Puerto Rico.: Imprenta del Gobierno de Puerto Rico, 1948.

Hostos, Eugenio María de, *Obras Completas, Tomo XII, Forjando el porvenir americano*, Vol. I. San Juan, Puerto Rico: ICP, 1969.

Iglesias de Pagán, *Igualdad, El obrerismo en Puerto Rico*. Palencia de Castilla, España: Ediciones Juan Ponce de León, 1973.

Iglesias Pantín, Santiago, *Luchas emancipadoras (Crónicas de Puerto Rico) (1910-1917)*. 2da. Ed. San Juan, Puerto Rico: Imprenta Venezuela, 1958-62.

———. *Gobierno propio.¿Para quién?* San Juan, P. R.: Typographical Union Label, 1907. 135 p. Informe de la Convención de la American Federation of Labor.

Kedward, Roderick, *Los anarquistas*. Barcelona, España: Ediciones Nanta, S.A., 1970.

Kriegel, Annie, *Las internacionales obreras*. Barcelona, España: Ediciones Martínez Roca, S.A., 1972.

Kropotkin, Piotr, *La conquista del pan*. Barcelona, España: Editorial Mateu, 1971.

Limon de Arce, José, *Arecibo histórico, Vol. I*. Manatí, Puerto Rico: Editorial Ángel Rosado, 1938.

López Tuero, Fernando, *La mujer*. San Juan, Puerto Rico: Tipografía del Boletín Mercantil, 1893.

Malatesta, Errico, *La anarquía*. Bilbao, España: Edita Zero, S.A., 1978.

———. *Hacia una nueva humanidad*. Brasil: Edicoes Proa, 1969.

Malato, Carlos, *Filosofía del anarquismo*. Madrid, España: Ediciones Júcar, 1978.

Marx, Karl, *Manuscritos: economía y filosofía*. Madrid, España: Alianza Editorial, 1977.

Montseny, Federica, *¿Qué es el anarquismo?* Barcelona: Editorial La Gaya Ciencia, 1976.

Mormino, Gary and George E. Pozzetta. *The Immigrant World of Ybor City, Italians and their Latin Neighbors in Tampa, 1885-1995*. Florida: University Press of Florida, 1987.

Negrón Muñoz, Ángela, *Mujeres de Puerto Rico, desde el principio de la colonización hasta el primer tercio del Siglo XX*. San Juan, Puerto Rico: Imprenta Venezuela, 1935.

Nettlau, Max, Miguel Bakunin, *La Internacional y la Alianza en España*. New York: Iberama Publishing Co., Inc., 1971.

Oranich Magda, *¿Qué es feminismo?* Barcelona, España: Editorial La Gaya Ciencia, 1976.

Osuna, Juan José, *A History of Education in Puerto Rico*. Río Piedras, Puerto Rico: Editorial de la Universidad de Puerto Rico, 1949.

Pagán, Bolívar, *El sufragio femenino*. San Juan, Puerto Rico: 1924.

Primelles, León, *Crónica cubana*, 1915-1918. La Habana, Cuba: Editorial Lex, 1955.

Punkerslut, "Francisco Ferrer y la Guardia (1859-1909)" in *The Anarchist Encyclopedia*. http://recollectionbooks.com/bleed/FerrerFrancisco.htm (retrieved July 11, 2005).

Pyziur, Eugene, *The Doctrine of Anarchism of Michael A. Bakunin*. Chicago, Ill.: A Gateway Edition, 1968.

Quintero Rivera, A.G., ed., *Lucha obrera en Puerto Rico*. Río Piedras, Puerto Rico: CEREP, 1972.

Randall, Margaret, ed., *Las mujeres*. México: Siglo XXI, 1970.

Rivera de Álvarez, Josefina, *Diccionario de literatura puertorriqueña, Tomo I*. San Juan, Puerto Rico: ICP, 1970.

Rivero Muñiz, Jose, *The Ybor City Story, 1885-1954*. Tampa, Florida, 1976.

Romeral, Ramón del, *Catecismo socialista*. San Juan de Puerto Rico: Imprenta de L. Labrador, 1905.

Rosario Natal, Carmelo, *La juventud de Luis Muñoz Marín*. Hato Rey, Puerto Rico: Master Typesetting de Puerto Rico, Inc., 1976.

Silén, Juan Ángel, *Apuntes para la historia del movimiento obrero puertorriqueño*. Río Piedras, Puerto Rico: Editorial Cultural, 1978.

Sifre de Loubriel, Estela, *Catálogo de extranjeros residentes en Puerto Rico en el Siglo XIX*. San Juan, Puerto Rico: ICP, 1973.

Skirda, Alexander, *Facing the Enemy: A History of Anarchist Organization from Proudhon to May 1968*. California: AK Press, 2000.

Solá, Mercedes, *Feminismo, Estudio sobre su aspecto social, económico y político*. San Juan, Puerto Rico: Cantero, Fernández & Co., Inc., 1922.

Tapia y Rivera, Alejandro, *El bardo de Guamaní, ensayos literarios*. La Habana, Cuba: Imprenta del Tiempo, 1882.

Torres, Alfonso, *Solidaridad*. San Juan, Puerto Rico: Unión Tipográfica, 1905.

Unión de Tipógrafos Núm. 422, *Páginas del obrero, colección de artículos para conmemorar el 1ro de mayo*, Imp. La Protesta, Mayagüez, 1904.

Valle-Ferrer, Norma, *Luisa Capetillo*. San Juan, Puerto Rico, Author's Edition, 1975.

Vega, Bernardo, *Memorias de Bernardo Vega*, César Andreu Iglesias, ed. San Juan, Puerto Rico: Ediciones Huracán, 1977.

———. *Memoirs of Bernardo Vega. A Contribution to the History of the Puerto Rican Community in New York*. New York: Monthly Review Press, 1984.

Wollstonecraft, Mary, *Vindication of the Rights of Woman*. England: Penguin Books, 1975.

Woodcock, George, *Anarchism, A History of Libertarian Ideas and Movements*. New York: The World Publishing Co., 1962.

Zayas, Nancy and Juan Ángel Silén, editors, *La mujer en la lucha hoy*. San Juan, Puerto Rico: Ediciones Kikirikí, 1972.

Articles

Alonso, Rafael, "Federación Libre de los Trabajadores de Puerto Rico," *Justicia*, 30 de septiembre de 1916, p. 2.

———. "Federación Libre de los Trabajadores de Puerto Rico," *Justicia*, 23 de septiembre de 1916, Año II, No. 95, p. 2.

———. "Anarquistas," *El Deber*, 3 de septiembre de 1913, p. 2.

Armiño, Franca de, "¿Por qué la mujer puertorriqueña debe intervenir en el gobierno de su país?," *Justicia*, s.f., p. 5.

Baldoni, Lola, "A la mujer," *La Mujer*, Año I, Núm. 2, 8 de marzo de 1894, p. 2.

Blanco Díaz, G. "Una flor sobre una tumba," *Unión Obrera*, 6 de mayo de 1922, p. 2.

Callejas, F., Billiken (pseudonym), "Venus con pantalones," *La Prensa*, La Habana, Cuba, martes, 27 de julio de 1915, p. 8.

Casado R., José, "A la malograda Luisa Capetillo," Santo Domingo, *Justicia*, Año II, No. 320, 29 de mayo de 1922, n. p.

Capetillo, Luisa, "La mujer," *Voces de Liberación*. Buenos Aires: Editorial Lux, 1921, pp. 4-6.

———. "Huelga en Patillas," Letter to Julio Aybar, *Unión Obrera*, Año 18, No. 35, 11 de febrero de 1918, n. p.

Celia, "La mujer puertorriqueña," *La Mujer*, 28 de marzo de 1894, Año 1, Núm. 3, Humacao, P.R., p. 2.

Combas Guerra, Eliseo, "En torno a la fortaleza," *El Mundo*, jueves, 11 de abril de 1974, p. 5-A.

Combas, Don, "Prudencio Rivera Martínez," *El Mundo*, 12 de octubre de 1963, p. 2 – Suplemento Sabatino.

"Como debe procederse," sobre el ingreso de 320 niños a la Beneficencia, *El Criterio Libre*, 3 de julio de 1899, n. p.

Cruz Monclova, Lidio, "El movimiento de las ideas en el Puerto Rico del Siglo XIX, *Boletín de la Academia Puertorriqueña de la Lengua Española*, Segundo y Tercer Trimestres de 1974. San Juan, Puerto Rico, 1974, n. p.

"De todo un poco, anarquismo," *El Criterio Libre*, 14 de agosto de 1899. p. 3.

Detenido, Pedro, "'Sobre Ideas,' poema dedicado a Luisa Capetillo," *Unión Obrera*, San Juan, Puerto Rico, 15 de noviembre de 1917.

"Doctrina perniciosa," *El Criterio Libre*, 19 de julio de 1899, p. 2.

"El caso de la mujer con traje masculino en la corte correccional; Luisa Capetillo fue absuelta después de un curioso interrogatorio," *El Heraldo de Cuba*, La Habana, Cuba, martes, 27 de julio de 1915, p. 12.

"El movimiento feminista se abre paso en la isla," *El Mundo*, domingo, 17 de abril de 1927, p. 1.

"El sufragio de la mujer," *Justicia*, 6 de septiembre de 1920, p. 14.

"Entrevista con Luisa Capetillo," *Porto Rico Progress*, 13 de julio de 1912, p. 7.

Eulate Sanjurjo, Carmela, "Influencia de la mujer," *La Mujer*, 24 de abril de 1894, pp. 1-2, Año 1, Núm. 5.

————. "La mujer," *La Mujer*, Año 1, Núm. 1, Humacao, Puerto Rico, 21 de febrero de 1894, p. 2.

"Falleció Luisa Capetillo," *El Tiempo, Diario Progresista de las Antillas*, San Juan, Puerto Rico, 11 de abril de 1922, n. p.

Freeman, Elizabeth, "Labores manuales en Puerto Rico," *Justicia*, 18 de abril de 1921, n. p.

Gabler, Hedda (pseudonym – Mercedes Negrón Muñoz), "Hablan las mujeres," *Juan Bobo*, 3 de 1917, p. 36.

García Calderón, José M., "Luisa Capetillo," *Noticias del Trabajo*, mayo-junio de 1969, n. p.

García, Gervasio, *Primeros fermentos de organización obrera en Puerto Rico: 1873-1898*. Río Piedras, Puerto Rico: CEREP, mimeographed copy, 1974.

García, Osvaldo, "Evocar para vivir. San Juan en el recuerdo de Agusty," Puerto Rico Ilustrado, *El Mundo*, 17 de septiembre de 1989, pp. 6-7.

"Información policíaca, vestida de hombre," *El Mundo*, domingo 25 de julio de 1915, p. 14.

Josefina, "Sobre el mismo tema," *La Mujer*, Humacao, Puerto Rico, 28 de marzo de 1894, Año 1, Núm. 3, pp. 2-3.

"La Asociación Feminista Popular de Puerto Rico," *Justicia*, 3 de enero de 1920, n. p.

"La huelga de Patillas," *Unión Obrera*, San Juan, Puerto Rico, 4 de febrero de 1918, n. p.

"La independencia política es negativa; Cuando no existe la libertad económica," *Justicia*, 14 de marzo de 1921, p. 16.

"La muerte de Luisa Capetillo," *El Imparcial*, miércoles, 12 de abril de 1922, n. p.

"La última nota, una brava hembra...," *La Lucha*, La Habana, Cuba, Año 31, Núm. 207, lunes 26 de julio de 1915, p. 2.

"Labor del intelecto y del músculo," *Justicia*, 14 de junio de 1920, pp. 10-11.

"Las excentricidades de una anarquista," *El Día*, La Habana, Cuba, 26 de julio de 1915, p. 1.

"Las mujeres tendrán voto," *Justicia*, 12 de julio de 1920, p. 16.

"Luisa Capetillo," *Unión Obrera*, Mayagüez, Puerto Rico, jueves, 16 de noviembre de 1911, n. p.

"Luisa Capetillo fue arrestada anoche," *Heraldo de Cuba*, Habana, Cuba, Año II, Núm. 206, domingo, 25 de julio de 1915, p. 1.

"Luisa Capetillo ha fallecido," *Unión Obrera*, jueves, 13 de abril de 1922, p. 1.

"Luisa Capetillo ha muerto...," *El Mundo*, martes, 11 de abril de 1922, p. 1.

"Luisa Capetillo," *Justicia*, Año 9, No. 314, San Juan, P.R., 17 de abril de 1922, p. 3.

"Luisa Capetillo," *La Democracia*, San Juan de Puerto Rico, 11 de abril de 1922, n. p.

"Luisa Capetillo, protagonista de una película cómica," *El Mundo*, Cuba, Año XVI, Núm. 5214, martes, 27 de julio de 1915, p. 10.

"Luisa Capetillo" en *Yo misma fui mi ruta: La mujer en la historia de Puerto Rico*. Centro de Investigaciones Sociales, Universidad de Puerto Rico, 1983, pp. 62-65.

"Murió Luisa Capetillo," *El Regionalista, Diario Unionista*, Arecibo, 11 de abril de 1922, n. p.   •

Negrón Muñoz, Angela, "Conversando con las principales feministas del país," *El Mundo*, domingo 22 de marzo de 1931, n. p.

Ojeda, Félix, "Verdades completas. Quien fue Luisa Capetillo," *Pueblo*, Año 25, No. 3, noviembre de 1973, n. p.

"Organización: reunión de damas obreras," *El Criterio Libre*, 7 de julio de 1899, p. 3.

Picó, Isabel, "Apuntes preliminares para el estudio de la mujer puertorriqueña y su participación en las luchas sociales de principios del Siglo XX," in *La mujer en América Latina*, Tomo XX, México: Editorial Sep-/Setentas, 1975, pp. 98-113.

Prado, Margarita del, "El feminismo y la religión," *Heraldo de la Mujer*, 30 de junio de 1919, p. 20.

Reglamento de la Asociación de Damas para la Instrucción de la Mujer, Puerto Rico: Imprenta del Boletín Mercantil, 1886, n. p.

"¡Reventón!," *El Criterio Libre*, julio 10 de 1899, n. p.

Ríos Ocaña, Manuel, "La muerte de Luisa Capetillo," *La Correspondencia*, San Juan de Puerto Rico, 12 de abril de 1922, n. p.

Rivera, A., "Por las costureras", *Justicia*, 7 de junio de 1921, n. p.

Rivera de Alvarado, Carmen, "La contribución de la mujer al desarrollo de la nacionalidad puertorriqueña," in *La mujer en la lucha hoy*, Nancy Zayas and Juan Ángel Silén, editors, San Juan, Puerto Rico: Ediciones Kikirikí, 1972, pp. 37-47.

Rivera Quintero, Marcia, "Política educativa y trabajo femenino 1898-1930," *En Rojo, Claridad*, del 24 al 30 de junio de 1977, pp. 10-11.

———. "La incorporación de la mujer al trabajo asalariado en las primeras décadas,"*En Rojo, Claridad*, del 17 al 23 de junio de 1977, p. 10.

———. "La mujer puertorriqueña en los procesos económicos y sociales del siglo XX (1)," *En Rojo, Claridad*, del 10 al 16 de junio de 1977, pp. 8-9.

Roqué de Duprey, Ana, "Deberá ser limitada la instrucción de la mujer," Primera Parte, *La Mujer*, Humacao, Puerto Rico, 8 de marzo de 1894, Año 1, Núm. 2, p. 1.

———. "Nuestro Programa," *La Mujer*, Humacao, Puerto Rico, 21 de febrero de 1894, p. 1.

"Tabaqueros triunfantes", *El Deber*, viernes, 11 de julio de 1913, Año 1, Núm. 9, p. 1.

Tirado, Amílcar, "Notas biográficas sobre Luisa Capetillo," Centro de Estudios Puertorriqueños, Hunter College *Newsletter*, June 1986, pp. 12–14, 29.

Torres, Pilar, "Para combatir la explotación del comercio," *Justicia*, 12 de julio de 1920, p. 12.

Valle-Ferrer, Norma, "Anarquismo y feminismo: la ideología de cuatro mujeres latino-americanas de principios del Siglo XX," *Revista Cultura, Instituto de Cultura Puertorriqueña*, San Juan, Puerto Rico, junio de 2004, pp. 92-99.

———. "La primera en liberarse," *La Hora*, 25 de abril al 1ro de mayo de 1974, pp. 12-13.

———. "Primeros fermentos de lucha femenina en Puerto Rico," *Revista del Instituto de Cultura Puertorriqueña*, San Juan, Puerto Rico, Núm. 84, julio-sep., 1979, pp. 15-19.

———. "Feminism and Its Influence on Women's Organizations in Puerto Rico," in *The Puerto Rican Woman*, Edna Acosta Belén, ed. New York: Praeger Publishers, 1979 (1st ed.), 1986 (2nd ed.).

———. "Luisa Capetillo (1879-1922), una herejía en la sociedad puertorriqueña," *Caribe*, año IV-V, Núm. 5-6, 1983-84, pp. 3-34.

———. "Luisa Capetillo," in "Lost Women," *Ms. Magazine*, New York, January 1975, p. 58.

———. "El teatro de Luisa Capetillo," *Revista del Ateneo Puertorriqueño*, San Juan, Puerto Rico, marzo-junio del 1985, p. 38.

———. "La voz dramática de Luisa Capetillo," *Revista del Instituto de Cultura Puertorriqueña*, San Juan, Puerto Rico, Núm. 94, oct.-dic. de 1986, pp. 21–24.

Vernet, Madeleine, "Sur l'amour libre," in *La Mère Educatrice*, Paris, France, *Troisiéme Année* (1919-20), pp. 83-87; Quatriéme Année (1920-1921), p. 7.

Documents

National Archives of Puerto Rico

—Records from Non-profit Organizations
Acción Liberal de Mujeres Votantes, Expediente de Incorporación (E.I.) #508.
(Liberal Action Women Voters, Document of Incorporation #508)
Asociación Feminista Educativa, E.I. #317.
(Feminist Educational Association, Document of Incorporation #317)
Gremio de Damas de Patillas, E.I. sin numerar (1904).
(Women's Guild of Patillas, Document of Incorporation, no number, 1904)
Liga Social Sufragista, E.I. #236.
(Social Sufragist League, Document of Incorporation, #236)
Unión de Despalilladoras de Tabaco de Arecibo, E.I. #347.
(Tobacco Leaf Strippers Union of Arecibo, Document of Incorporation #347)
Unión de Mujeres Puertorriqueñas, E.I. #809.
(Puerto Rico Women's Union, Document of Incorporation #809)

—Police Records, Puerto Rico
Log Book, Ceiba, 1917-1918.

—Archives of the Santa Catedral of Arecibo.
Baptismal Records
Perón, Luisa Margarita, Libro 40, Folio 57.

—Archives of the *Federación Libre de Trabajadores* (Free Libertarian Federation of Puerto Rican Workers)
    Luisa Capetillo, letters.
    Santiago Iglesias Pantín, letters.

—Demographic Registry and Bureau of Vital Statistics of Puerto Rico
    Death Certificates
    Capetillo, Luisa, Libro 36, Folio 350, Acta 350.

Other Documents

Manuela Ledesma Capetillo, Luisa Capetillo's daughter, gave me several letters written by Gregorio Ledesma, Capetillo's son, and his father, Manuel Ledesma. She also gave me a small notebook with notes written by Capetillo and other miscellaneous memorabilia.

Personal interviews

These interviews are preserved on audio cassettes:

Nadal Barreto. Tobacco worker, friend of Capetillo. Arecibo, 1974.

Julie Capetillo de Fair. Capetillo's niece. San Juan, 1975.

Ángel Gandía. Capetillo's co-worker. Manatí, 1974.

Manuela Ledesma Capetillo. Capetillo's daughter. Carolina, 1974.

José Rosa. Capetillo's son-in-law. Manatí, 1974.